MISSIONS IN THE
THIRD MILLENNIUM

MISSIONS IN THE
THIRD MILLENNIUM

21 Key Trends for the 21st Century

STAN GUTHRIE

paternoster
press

First published 2000 by Paternoster Press

06 05 04 03 02 01 00   7 6 5 4 3 2 1

Paternoster Press is an imprint of Paternoster Publishing,
PO Box 300, Carlisle, Cumbria CA3 0QS, UK
and Paternoster Publishing USA
Box 1047, Waynesboro, GA 30830–2047
www.paternoster-publishing.com

British Library Cataloguing in Publication Data

A catalogue record for this book is available from the British Library

ISBN 1–84227–042–7

Typeset by Waverley Typesetters, Galashiels
Cover design by Campsie
Printed and bound in the USA by
RR Donnelley and Sons, Harrisonburg, VA

To Christine

Acknowledgments

The byline is one of the most misleading elements in all of literature. No book was ever written alone. Many of the chapters in this volume began as articles for *Evangelical Missions Quarterly* and *World Pulse*, published by the Evangelism and Missions Information Service of the Billy Graham Center at Wheaton College. Thanks to Jim Reapsome, the editor for much of my time with EMIS, for modeling both a clear-eyed journalistic realism and a genuine compassion for people. Thanks, Jim, for your patience. I appreciate the rest of the team there, as well: Ken Gill, Jean Warren, Karen Rummel, Dona Diehl, Deb Ferguson, and Gary Corwin. Through lots of ups and downs, you all have taught me much about my work and my life. Thanks also to John Orme and Paul McKaughan for their perceptive comments about earlier versions of the manuscript; to Pieter Kwant for his promotion of the book; to Patrick Johnstone for his advice; to Dave Mays, Doug McConnell, Jon Bonk, Evvy Campbell, Darrow Miller, Dave Hesselgrave, Ted Yamamori, and all the rest for their encouragement; and to Isobel Stevenson for her sharp editing. Most of all, thanks to Christine, Laura, and Peter, who put up with stacks of unwashed dishes, piles of unopened mail, and constricted family time so that I could pursue this obsession to its conclusion.

Contents

Foreword   xi

Introduction   xv

I. THE HOME ARENA

1. New Paradigms for Churches and Agencies   3
2. Supporting National Workers   10
3. Missionary Malaise   18
4. Missionary Care   29
5. Theological Drift   37
6. Women in Missions   45

II. THE STRATEGIC ARENA

7. The 10/40 Window   57
8. Year 2000 Evangelism Plans   64
9. Prayer as Warfare   74
10. The Short-Term Missions Explosion   85
11. Partnerships   93
12. Contextualization   101
13. Missions as Process vs. Missions as Project   112

Contents

14.	Tentmaking	117
15.	Holism	123

III. THE OVERSEAS CHURCH ARENA

16.	The Globalization of Christianity	133
17.	The Charismatic Boom	139
18.	The Maturing of International Missionary Movements	146

IV. THE GLOBAL ARENA

19.	Global Culture	157
20.	Radical Reactions	167
21.	Persecution and Religious Liberty	178

V. CONCLUSION

22.	What's Next?	191

Appendix	200
Notes	206

Foreword

One can only be grateful for an invitation to write the foreword to a book as fine and as full of promise as this one. Stan Guthrie, an editor of two internationally acclaimed mission periodicals, has produced a volume which is lucid, insightful, and constructively provocative.

Provocation has its rightful place, for it can produce sparks, sparks can kindle a flame, and a flame sheds light! Guthrie correctly points out that missionary action takes place within ever-changing contexts. The future to which the book's title points is simply an extension of the past, on a continuum intersected by the present. And it is only in the present that incarnational Christian mission can take place. That is why it is both appropriate and essential that Guthrie should address issues at the very heart of contemporary mission theory and practice – timeless yet current issues relating to missionary motivation and methods, financial support and pastoral care, personal relationships in both familiar and cross-cultural settings, and huge challenges arising from local contexts and global trends. Not only do these contexts and trends shape and define contemporary human beings, including missionaries, but they also constitute the carriers of sinister elements that a Christian missionary must attempt to recognize and resist.

This volume will enjoy a global readership, and it is safe to say that its reading will contribute to a healthy jettisoning of several false or merely outdated assumptions that are often implicit in our thinking about missions. For example, the idea that North America (especially the United States) continues to be the heartland of Christianity will not withstand a careful reading of this book. The Christian "center of gravity" is no longer the comfortable West, whose Christian confidence has been steadily leavened by the subliminal agnosticism that almost always accompanies prosperity (Rev. 3:14–20).

The vitality that marks the most dynamically missionary churches is today most readily observed in the great continents of Africa, Asia, and South America. That this should be so is not surprising, since Christianity has seldom, if ever, remained healthy and vigorous within rich, dominant societies. The North American component of the global Christian missionary force is, accordingly, a steadily diminishing proportion of the whole. In 1900 there were an estimated 16,000 missionaries, most of these from Europe, Great Britain, and North America. Today, if we use David Barrett's more expansive definition for foreign missionaries (not limited to those who earn their living as missionaries), the total number is some 420,000, with a mere 12–15 percent of these hailing from Western lands.

The assumption that most missionaries are employees of entities known as mission societies, modeled along corporate lines, will also fare badly as a result of the author's perceptive discussion of such bread-and-butter issues as partnerships, tentmaking, globalization, and short-term missions. Observers of global Christian trends now believe that a vast majority of missionaries work more or less spontaneously, as informal or formal extensions of local communities of faith, with little or no organic link to the European tribal Christianity that we Westerners have come to identify as the norm. Western cognitive maps and vocabularies have yet to catch up with this reality, since they often reflect an earlier era when "missionaries" were American or Europeans who went "overseas" to the less civilized (now read "developed") parts of the globe.

Furthermore, most missionaries today derive from denominations whose names do not appear in many of our encyclopedias and handbooks. These missionaries are lay, not ordained, and they tend to be associated with charismatic or Pentecostal churches. In 1900, the total number of distinct and organizationally separate denominational bodies in the world stood at 1,880. Today the estimate stands at more than 30,000, a majority of these outside of North America and Europe.

Such facts, constituting a kind of backdrop to Guthrie's treatment of the charismatic movement and religious persecution, are a reminder that it is now and always has been the poor who respond with irrepressibly contagious joy to the good news. But this itself poses serious "who," "where," and "how" questions for contemporary missions – questions implicit in Guthrie's chapters on contextualization, holism, and international missionary movements.

Thoughtful readers will be well served by this book. The discussion questions at the end of each chapter make the book a natural for college seminars, mission discussion groups, and Sunday school classes. I only wish that such a book had been available to me when I taught undergraduate mission seminars!

JONATHAN J. BONK
Director, Overseas Ministries Study Center
Editor, *International Bulletin of Missionary Research*
New Haven, Connecticut
August, 2000

Introduction

The South Asian parents of an infant boy took him to a Hindu guru for a blessing and for advice about an auspicious name. For some reason, they ignored the guru's counsel and gave the boy a name that means "God's victory." A month or two later, the boy's Hindu nanny took the baby to her temple so that the priest could pronounce a blessing on him. But the priest refused, telling her, "I cannot do anything for this child. This one belongs to the Most High God."

The boy and his family, while living among numerous Hindu and Muslim neighbors, belonged to a people group that few Westerners even know exists – the Parsees. Parsees worship fire, pray to their ancestors, and follow a creed that can be summarized as "good thoughts, good words, good deeds." The world's estimated 3.5 million Parsees remain one of the least reached people groups, as they have been ever since a religious reformer named Zoroaster (or Zarathustra) founded the religion on the plains of Persia in the sixth century B.C. Among the prominent Parsees mentioned in the Bible are Cyrus, Darius, and the magi who worshiped the baby Jesus.

Eventually, the growing Parsee boy began praying and chanting at the Zoroastrian fire temple for hours and hours after his school day was over. In fact, he showed more promise in the religion than anyone in his family. During one of his visits, however, the boy realized that he should not pray to the fire or to the pictures of dead Parsees. Somehow, he knew that worshipping created things is idolatry. After several Parsee leaders failed to satisfactorily answer his probing questions, he decided never again to bow before those things.

Later, after a time of spiritual searching and experimentation, the young man went to a university in the West for graduate studies. Unknown to his Parsee friends, Christians in the area began providing him with answers. One gave him a Bible and took him to church. The pastor there was always available to field his insistent questions.

There is a time in every spiritual seeker's life for questions. But there is also a time for decisions. Soon, the young man knew what he had to do, and he received Christ. He says simply about his conversion, "I found the answer and was satisfied when I found Christ."

Despite opposition and ridicule, this Parsee believer is now actively engaged in reaching his people for Jesus. Only about thirty of them have a saving relationship with Jesus. Once highly esteemed by the Parsee leaders, this young man is now the object of ridicule and threats.

"This charade of being a Christian missionary doesn't befit you," one Parsee leader told him. "You are not preaching to some backward, ignorant community. You are preaching to Parsee-Zarathushtis, an intelligent people who are 100 percent literate.

"Our advice to you once again is that you please cease this charade immediately, return to your fold at once, show some remorse for the harm you have brought to the good name of your people, and continue to be a good Parsee-Zarathushti. If you do not have the courage to do so, practice whatever faith you like in your own home without trying to convert another Parsee. If you persist in your current activities, you will find that the Parsees will not take it lying down but will fight you all the way."

But for the Parsee believer whose name means "God's victory" the approval of the risen Savior counts for much more than acceptance among his people, or even his own life. Though the temptation is strong to simply privatize his faith, he will not stop doing his potentially dangerous work. "There are too many souls dying for me to do that," he said. "What I do is by an act of my will, by necessity. I make myself do the things that I have to do because there are so many souls dying without the Lord."[1]

Mission, the outward focus of people who want to share the good news of Jesus Christ with peoples who don't necessarily want to hear about him, has always been God's idea first. Jesus told his fearful disciples the night he was betrayed, "You did not choose me, but I chose you and appointed you to go and bear fruit – fruit that will last" (John 15:16a). Mission, when done right, is done not only in Christ's authority but in his very presence. As the resurrected Lord told his disciples before departing for his heavenly coronation, "All authority in heaven and on earth has been given to me. Therefore go and make disciples of all nations, baptizing them in the name of the Father and of the Son and of the Holy Spirit, and teaching them to obey everything I have commanded you. And surely I am with you always, to the very end of the age" (Matt. 28:18b–20). This has rightly come to be known as the Great Commission.

Yet, despite this assurance, the church has always faced the temptation of silence. Opposition has confronted cross-cultural workers throughout the church's two millennia of existence. But whether it has been the Apostle Peter informing the religious authorities in Jerusalem that he would obey God rather than man, or William Carey telling the hyper-Calvinists of the day of their responsibility to make disciples around the world, or "God's victory" doggedly pursuing the Parsees in spite of insult and threat, missions has succeeded when God's people have overcome their natural inertia to proclaim the Good News to a world hostile or indifferent to Christ.

The fruit of the worldwide evangelistic task is unmistakably impressive. A third of the world's people call themselves Christians. Christianity, in all its forms, has become the world's most global faith. Followers of Jesus are present in every country. Countless lives have been transformed by the risen and reigning Christ, especially in the 20th century.

Evangelical Christianity is the world's fastest-growing major religion in terms of conversion growth, and signs of this are evident even in areas traditionally closed to missionaries. In the Islamic world, Muslims are responding to the gospel in small but significant ways. Thousands of Muslims in North Africa have become followers of Christ in the last decade. The evangelical agency Interdev reports great strides in forming strategic evangelism partnerships to reach Muslims with the gospel. Middle East Media reports surging interest in Christian literature. Meanwhile, in Indonesia, the scene of organized Muslim attacks against Christians since 1998, the overall church may have grown to 20 million people – far above the official estimate of 13 to 15 million.

Latin America's active evangelical contingent now numbers 60 million people, two-thirds of whom are Pentecostals able to reach the region's poor and disenfranchised masses. Latin evangelicals are taking their missions responsibilities seriously, too. Increasingly they see themselves as a missions force rather than a mission field. Latins are particularly eager to win Muslims to Christ and are training to do so ever more effectively. Meanwhile, early in the 1990s, the Quechua people of Bolivia were said to be largely unreached with the gospel. Today the evangelical movement among them numbers more than 50,000. A decade ago the Bellavista prison in Colombia was one of the most violent and dehumanizing places on earth. Today, amid a continuing revival, it is the site of a Bible school.

In Europe, where the light of active evangelism has been dimmed for decades, there are signs of hope. At the Mission '99 conference in the Netherlands, some 1,000 of the 7,000 young people in attendance committed to pursuing ministry. In Germany, hundreds of evangelical churches have been planted between 1988 and 1995.

In the countries of the former Soviet Union, the Alliance for Saturation Church Planting and the CoMission have reported encouraging results in spreading the gospel. The former, a co-operative effort of churches and 35 agencies, reports that local church planters have started 2,500 new churches in four years, including 767 in 1998. In Ukraine, Light of the Gospel, a ministry launched during the reign of the communists, is sending workers to Kazakhstan and elsewhere.

In China, the church has multiplied from about 5 million when the communists took power in 1949 to anywhere from 30 to 60 million today; revival continues despite opposition in Henan province. India, where more than 140 religiously motivated attacks against Christians by Hindus have been recorded over the last several years, is the home turf of a vibrant and brave missionary movement of 200 Indian agencies and several thousand missionaries to tribal peoples.

African Christianity continues its amazing growth. More than 200,000 people in Chad made public decisions for Christ in outreaches between 1993 and 1998. Ethiopia, with large numbers of nominally Orthodox Christians and Muslims, has seen its evangelical community increase from .08 percent of the population in 1962 to 15.5 percent in 1998. Sudan, site of some of the worst persecution of Christians on earth, has seen perhaps the creation of a million more Bible-believing Christians in the south since 1982.

And yet, too often, the missions movement has failed, usually because the church has failed. At the dawn of the third millennium, the task ("go and make disciples of all nations," Matt. 28:19) remains undone.

While there is much excitement about reaching "unreached people groups" with the gospel, the reality is more sobering. The AD2000 and Beyond Movement's revised Joshua Project lists 1,595 unreached people groups.[2] Some 1,118 of them have no church of 100 people; 537 don't even have a team of church planters yet. However, this list is just a beginning. Some 4,000 groups, not just 1,595, have no viable Christian witness, according to missions statistician David Barrett.[3]

The proportion of the world's population that is unevangelized came down dramatically last century. The proportion that had not heard a gospel presentation shrank from 50.2 percent in 1900, to 44.3 percent in 1970, to 29.5 percent in 1990, to 25.7 percent in 2000. The proportion is expected to decline further to 21.6 percent in 2025, according to Barrett and Todd Johnson in the January 2000 *International Bulletin of Missionary Research*. Yet there are an estimated 1.556 billion people in the world who have never heard the gospel. Their ranks are expected to increase to 1.687 billion by 2025.[4] The number of people born in the non-Christian world grows by 129,000 a day, or 47 million a year, according to Barrett.[5] Clearly, if fulfilling the Great Commission depends on seeing that everyone hears, it is nowhere near completion.

As missions historian Will Norton, Sr., has said, "The fact that . . . 1.5 billion people are unevangelized as the third millennium is upon us is evidence enough that the church of the Lord Jesus Christ has not yet complied with the original directive: '. . . you shall be my witnesses unto the uttermost part of the earth.'"[6]

This book has been written with that fact in mind. This volume is both descriptive and prescriptive. Not only do I want to chart the major trends and make some predictions about missions in the third millennium, I hope to offer some suggestions to help students, churches, missionaries, agencies, and Christians from outside the West be more effective in our common task of carrying out the Great Commission.

Today might well be labeled the Age of Uncertainty in evangelical missions. As befits our postmodern times, we are buffeted by doubts and criticism from both inside and outside the camp. While vigorous questioning of old verities is often healthy, we often seem paralyzed with fear. Will we be seen as colonialists? Absolutists? Sexists? Are mission agencies passé? Should tentmakers and short-termers be given the reins instead? Or maybe churches? Should missionaries focus more on humanitarian ministries instead of just evangelism? Can't good Hindus, Buddhists, and Muslims be saved in their own religions?

For convenience and clarity, I have divided this book into four main sections dealing with the home arena, the strategic arena, the overseas church arena, and the global arena. Then chapter 22 summarizes the book and takes a final look ahead. While these categories are not exhaustive, they provide a fairly reliable framework for examining current issues in missions. There is some unavoidable overlap of subjects in a few of the chapters, but I have tried to keep this to a minimum. For example, the tendency of some Western churches to support only "nationals" (chapter 2) is bound up with the globalization of Christianity (chapter 16), as well as with the West's own missionary malaise (chapter 3). While the topics are related, each deserves a full treatment. For readers who want to dig deeper, I have included suggestions for further reading, discussion questions that work well for individuals and groups, as well as end notes on my sources.

The book is meant to be wide-ranging in subject but not comprehensive in detail; accurate but not ivory tower; theological but not impractical. My aim is to examine current trends that will have continuing significance well into the next century in the light of biblical principles. I attempt to present a balanced assessment of each issue, neither Pollyannaish nor overly gloomy. Along the way, some missions fads and myths may be exploded for some readers. The intent, however, is not to create controversy but to dispel error and advance truth, as I see them. Obviously, I am not perfect and have much to learn. As time goes on, I expect to be proven wrong in some areas. Discerning readers will also see some of my own biases, which, I hope, are supported by the facts.

A constant theme of this volume is the need for the missions movement to return to the Book for its marching orders. If readers are encouraged to pray, support missions, and perhaps even go more effectively and faithfully, this book will have accomplished its mission.

Part I

THE HOME ARENA

Chapter 1

New Paradigms for Churches and Agencies

A missions elder from a megachurch told Sam Metcalf of Church Resource Ministries in Pasadena, California, why his church had decided to discontinue the ministry of a missionary. "We didn't approve of what the missionary was doing, so we told him that he and his family had to return to the States," the elder said. "After all, he's supported by us 100 percent. He's our missionary."

"But doesn't he work for an agency?" Metcalf asked. "Aren't they his employer and supervisor?"

"Yes," the elder replied, "but we pay the bill; the agency doesn't."[1]

Long-term missionary interest is bubbling in a lot of churches at the launch of the third millennium, and this raises important questions for all stakeholders as churches and agencies try on new roles in the missionary enterprise.

The can-do spirit

Churches, mobilized by the can-do entrepreneurial spirit of their business people, short-term vision trips by members, and the process of rubbing shoulders with increasingly multi-cultural neighbors, are becoming more and more creative in their attempts to obey Christ's Great Commission to make disciples among all nations. While overall missions interest seems static at best in North America, when measured by long-term workers sent and money spent (see chapter 3), on the local level some congregations are more creative and energized than ever.

There is no one way to "do" missions in the local church, though there are many wrong ways. Nor is there an ideal size to be effective. Tom Telford has compiled a list of missions-minded churches that includes everything from the 225-member Candia Congregational Church in Candia, New Hampshire, to megachurches like Wooddale Church in Eden Prairie, Minnesota, and the Elmbrook Church in Waukesha, Wisconsin.[2]

In his book *Missions in the 21st Century: Getting Your Church into the Game*, Telford lists nine elements for a top-flight program: an outward focus; 30 percent or more of the budget going to missions; a training program for candidates; missions education throughout the church's programs; sending its own people; concern and prayer for the lost; a pastor who leads in missions; assistance to other churches in missions; and a strong local evangelism program.[3]

The role of agencies

After reading the above list, one mission agency executive pointed out that working with sending organizations was conspicuously absent. For some churches, that omission is no oversight. Citing what they see as the high costs and ossified thinking of traditional missions agencies, a sizable bloc of churches, sometimes called megachurches for their size and clout, has decided to go it alone. In effect, they, either by themselves or as members of a larger association of like-minded churches, have decided to become their own agencies. Churches such as those that are members of the Willow Creek Association are now strategizing, training, deploying, and evaluating the success or failure of workers largely without the input of agencies. Of course, they risk making the same mistakes and relearning the very same lessons the agencies have over the decades – worst of all, needlessly.

Some churches refuse to send missionaries through outside agencies, in order to cut out the "middleman." Others, less radical, support only their own people, usually in part because of budgetary constraints. These churches don't like the high costs agencies say it takes to send missionaries these days and believe they can do it more cheaply. However, they will still sometimes avail themselves of mission-founded schools for missionary kids or other resources paid for by somebody else. Irritatingly, to the agencies, some of the high costs churches complain about are caused by things they demanded agencies provide for their people – such as pension funds and medical insurance.

"Another reason for the estrangement of these long-term partners is theological. Some in the church-only movement see the church, either locally or through denominational boards, as the only legitimate sender of missionaries."[4] Independent boards are seen as, at best, necessary evils, because the church hasn't got its missions act together. They are not given the same status as the church.

Most churches, however, are willing to dance with their long-time agency partners, who know the ropes when it comes to cross-cultural ministry, obtaining visas, and the thousand-and-one details associated with missions. Bethlehem Baptist is one that has chosen not to re-invent the wheel. Missions Pastor Tom Steller says, "I don't feel we have the time or expertise to do what a well-run agency can do."[5]

However, even the many congregations that choose to work with mission agencies now ask tougher, more probing questions of their long-time ministry partners than they did. Fading is the old paradigm of agencies simply harvesting the money and manpower of supportive and compliant churches. Agencies, so much a force in the modern missions movement since William Carey's day, are being forced to justify everything they do. Agencies have discovered that he who pays the piper calls the tune, even in missions.

Money matters

Raising support remains a formidable obstacle for many would-be missionaries thinking about going through traditional, independent agencies. The process can mean visiting scores of churches around the country, families in tow, and can last eighteen months, two years, or more. Some missionaries, who might be good in ministry but are bad at raising funds, never make it.

In response, a few very large churches have committed to providing full financial support to a smaller number of missionaries. For example, instead of paying a hundred missionaries $25 a month, the idea is to pay one worker $2,500 a month – saving wear and tear on the missionary and speeding the start of actual ministry. Other local churches, such as some in Indianapolis and Minneapolis/Saint Paul, have banded together in consortia, and agreed to support a pool of workers at significant financial levels. In exchange, the missionaries and candidates are expected to do ministry in these churches and get to know their church members.[6] For these churches, a five-minute Sunday night presentation once every four years just won't cut it anymore. This approach fits well with the baby boomer desire for personal, hands-on contact and involvement.

A downside to these kinds of concentrated support is the risk that supporting churches may splinter, close, or change their ministry focus. Such developments leave their workers far more vulnerable than those working under the old paradigm. If a church that provides all the support for a missionary collapses because of internal strife, that missionary must return home. However, if that church provides only a small fraction of his support, the ministry can go on.

A question of control

Another problem is that a church may decide, for whatever reason, that a missionary family no longer fits its strategic vision. One worker and his family doing Bible translation work among Muslims were forced to return to the USA after a supporting church's leadership decided to focus on church planting. (The missionary wondered how church planting could be done apart from the Bible, but that is a different story.)

When Paul Borthwick, a former minister of Grace Chapel in Lexington, Massachusetts, wrote an article entitled "What local churches are saying to mission agencies" in *Evangelical Missions Quarterly* (July 1999), Larry Sharp of UFM International penned a quick response, "What an agency leader would say to local churches" (January 2000). "Agencies and churches pull in different directions when it comes to missionary evaluation and accountability," says Jim Reapsome, editor-at-large for *World Pulse* and *Evangelical Missions Quarterly*. In a column he said churches want regular performance reports, more say in missionary deployment, up-to-date financial support information, pastoral care for missionaries, and current information on agency personnel needs. He says most agencies come up short in these areas. He likens churches and agencies to a team of horses pulling in different directions.

"For more than 40 years I have traveled with both horses, both as a pastor and as a member of several mission boards," Reapsome said. "I have listened to both sides and am amazed that they cannot find time to sit down and listen to one another with mutual respect, trust, and appreciation. They must get off the path of mutual criticism."[7]

While the dialogue between churches and agencies has been civil (for the most part), it has, at times, been painful. Like an employee writhing under a tough review from the boss, agencies have not always enjoyed all the questioning. But, slowly, they are learning to live with it. Those who embrace the creativity of churches, learn from it, and correct its excesses will prosper in the 21st century. For while the local church is not the only element the Lord of missions uses, it is the key one.

"Local churches are the key to world missions," stated Paul Beals, professor emeritus at Grand Rapids Baptist Seminary. "They are the source of missionary personnel, of financial support, and of informed prayer. They are the engine, under God, that drives world mission."[8]

Bethlehem Baptist Church, a large congregation in downtown Minneapolis, illustrates the point. BBC sent out its first missionary in 1890, but its overseas outreach program slowly slipped into dormancy. But in 1983 the speaker chosen for the missions conference was unable to come at the last minute, and the pastor was hastily inserted in his place. As he planned, prayed, and pored over the great missionary themes in the Bible, the pastor's heart was ignited for the glory of God around the world. That pastor's name was John Piper, the author of the instant missionary classic *Let the Nations Be Glad: The Supremacy of God in Missions.* Among its maxims: "Missions exists because worship doesn't."

Bethlehem caught his vision and began setting goals. The 1,100-member church invests part of its $580,000 missions budget in its own inner-city neighborhood helping the jobless become employable. In 1990 the church purposed to plant three churches by 2000. That goal has been met. Another was to send 200 church members as missionaries. That goal is still in process.[9]

Still, it hasn't taken the church long to turn things around. Missions mobilizer and agitator Tom Telford, on staff with United World Mission, has named Bethlehem among the top 21 missions-minded congregations in the USA.[10]

Tom Steller says simply, "Long-term missionary interest is bubbling strong again at BBC."[11]

FURTHER READING

"When local churches act like agencies," by Sam Metcalf, *Evangelical Missions Quarterly (EMQ)*, April 1993.

"What local churches are saying to mission agencies," by Paul Borthwick, *EMQ*, July 1999.

"What an agency leader would say to local churches," by Larry Sharp, *EMQ*, January 2000.

"Growing local church initiatives," by John Siewert, *Mission Handbook* (Monrovia: MARC, 1997).

"The right stuff: Former umpire calls 21 churches on the ball in missions involvement," by Deann Alford, *World Pulse*, 21 August 1998.

Missions in the 21st Century: Getting Your Church into the Game, by Tom Telford, with Lois Shaw (Wheaton: Harold Shaw Publishers, 1998).

"Mission societies: Are they biblical?" by Frank M. Severn, *EMQ*, July 2000.

God's Missionary People: Rethinking the Purpose of the Local Church, by Charles Van Engen (Grand Rapids: Baker, 1991).

DISCUSSION QUESTIONS

1. *Which do you think is God's primary means to spread the gospel – local churches, denominational mission boards, independent mission boards, or something else? Why?*

2. *What factors contribute to the high cost of missionary support? How can this cost be reduced?*

3. *Does your church work well with mission agencies, and vice versa?*

4. *What are some creative approaches your organization can use to engage in global ministry more effectively and more faithfully to the Scriptures?*

Chapter 2

Supporting National Workers

Jim Lo was a church-planting missionary in Zimbabwe in the 1980s who was convinced that the Africans he worked with needed to take a larger role in the ministry. He was disturbed by the paternalistic attitude that only Western missionaries could do the work, especially as he rubbed shoulders with seasoned African leaders. Others on the missions leadership team agreed. They thought that the main reason these Africans were not involved in starting churches was a lack of money. So the money (only $500 a month for one Zimbabwean, versus $1,250 for a Westerner) was allocated to the church for three paid workers.

Soon, however, giving in the churches that had already been started dried up. When Lo tried to find out why, one African told him, "If rich Americans can pay for salaries, they should also be able to pay for the needs of our church."

Ministry dried up, too, as church volunteers quickly came to believe that they also should be paid. Lo was told, "If the church in America can pay salaries for three men to do church planting, it should be able also to find money to pay us to teach Sunday school."

Church members also would not financially support the three church planters, calling them "missionary boys" who were not accountable to the church. Indeed, one of the three told Lo, "I only listen to the person who pays my salary."[1]

Part of a trend

Seeking the help of "nationals" is a growing trend in our world. Facing a shortage of employees with high-tech skills, Silicon Valley executives have for some time been lobbying for a loosening of restrictions on their ability to hire foreign professionals. Sometimes businesses, rather than recruiting internationally, simply move their operations to countries where the cost of labor is cheaper. Former billionaire presidential candidate Ross Perot famously complained that he heard a "giant sucking sound" because of a free trade agreement with Mexico. Other protectionist candidates such as Pat Buchanan have voiced similar concerns.

The North American missionary is apparently no more immune to globalization's disorienting new economic ground rules than the factory worker competing with "cheaper" workers in Mexico. Both missionaries and blue-collar employees are being forced to justify their existence. Not all are succeeding.

The numbers

The numbers are compelling, on one level. With travel, ministry expenses, pension funds, insurance, and schooling for the kids, annual missionary financial support levels can easily top $50,000, $75,000, or more, depending on place of service. Compare that to the $60 to $120 a month groups like Gospel For Asia claim it costs to pay for more culturally attuned native missionaries, and you might be tempted to wonder why there are any full-time career Westerners left. One US agency that financially supports overseas "missionaries" headlines its advertisements to American readers with the words, "Thank you for staying home." Taking a different tack, Chuck Bennett, the former president of Partners International, has stated, "Our Protestant mission enterprise is at a crossroad. Not because it has failed, but largely because it has succeeded."[2]

On one level, the statistics bear Bennett out. Until 1960, Christianity was still largely a Western faith. In 1960, about 58 percent of those who called themselves Christians were Westerners, according to missions researcher Patrick Johnstone. By 1990, this had fallen to 38 percent, as the gospel surged across large swathes of Asia, Africa, and Latin America[3] and as

the harvest tracked, and in many cases surpassed, world population growth trends.

"We still use terms like 'the mission field' that reflect the days
when northern Europe and North America were mostly Christian
and the rest of the world mostly non-Christian," Bennett, a
former missionary to Mexico, wrote in *Evangelical Missions
Quarterly*. "Today half of all Christians in the world, and
perhaps 70 percent of all evangelicals, live in these traditional
'mission fields,' but we continue to invest 90 percent of our
recruiting, training, and funding to send Western missionaries
to pretty much those same fields."[4]

The growth of the movement supporting non-Western
Christians is a post-World War II phenomenon. A 50-member
Coalition for the Support of Indigenous Ministries (COSIM) was
formed in 1998. Only a few of the member agencies, including
Gospel For Asia, Partners International, and Overseas Council,
had been around for at least two decades. Yet Gospel For Asia,
just one member of the relatively new movement, claims to
support 11,000 native missionaries.[5] COSIM has also identified
a network of some 225 North American organizations that aim
to support indigenous church planting, evangelism, relief and
development, leadership training, and theological education.

But on another level, the statistics on the worldwide missionary force are in dispute. What, after all, is a "missionary"?
Definitions vary. Johnstone, author of the standard missions
prayer guide, *Operation World*, warns against comparing
apples and oranges: "North Americans count only those working outside North America. . . . Europeans and Latin Americans
tend to count all working in cross-cultural agencies. Africans
and Asians usually count all sent to plant churches – whether
cross-culturally or not." Defining missionaries both as expatriates
serving as foreign missionaries (both cross-cultural and in a
near culture) and as nationals working within their own country,
Johnstone estimates the number of missionaries worldwide as
138,492, of whom some 64,378 are North American.[6] (Such
figures are imprecise and must be taken as they are intended, as
estimates.)

Weaknesses

CLC International (formerly Christian Literature Crusade), with its 700-person missionary force in 50 nations, is an example of the indigenization of missions. Its team comprises 600 locals working with 100 foreign missionaries. Yet, as Lewis Codington points out, there are still problems. For one thing, local workers have a different perspective. "The most serious problem we encounter is a lack of world vision. . . . When people are going back and forth to work in their own country and their entire world consists of what they see on their trip back and forth to work, they can lose sight of the bigger picture, and we find that there is a lack of awareness of the world harvest, which foreign missionaries tend to see much more clearly."[7]

Alex Araujo, a former executive with Partners International and a native of Brazil, also sounds a reluctant note of caution concerning his non-Western missions brethren even while he cheers them on. "Beware of glorious portrayals of the emerging non-Western missions movement," he says. "Though highly welcome and deserving of credit and encouragement, [it] is a mixed bag of good and bad, success and tragedy, and should not be idealized."[8]

William Taylor, director of the Missions Commission of the World Evangelical Fellowship (WEF) and a former missionary to Guatemala, similarly says that because of weaknesses in their sending, training, and shepherding bases, non-Western churches and mission agencies are often better at sending people out than keeping them on the field. He urges Christians to examine the reputation of non-Western missions organizations carefully before sending donations.[9] To overcome ignorance on the part of would-be Western supporters, churches and agencies should work with established networks and agencies that know their countries and can vouch for the integrity and effectiveness of would-be recipients. The WEF, COSIM, World Relief Corporation, and various national evangelical fellowships are good places to go for references and insights when undertaking this kind of ministry.

Many missionaries and agency executives are careful to distinguish between financially supporting overseas missionaries and supporting church workers. Supporting missionaries is necessary, because these workers go to where there are no churches that could pay them. Supporting church workers is another matter, for at least one study, done in Indonesia, indicates that churches generally grow better and have fewer problems if they pay their own pastors.

A specific example of this comes from one church in Latin America, where American missionaries chose a gifted young Christian from the country to become the pastor. Because the church had few financial resources, they paid his entire salary in the hope that as the church grew it would eventually be able to support him. Unfortunately, that never happened, and the pastor and his wife remained dependent on the missionaries. Later, the pastor was found to have been involved in a moral failure and to have physically abused his wife. When she was asked why she had said nothing about this abuse, the woman replied, "If I admitted that we were having problems, I feared that the missionaries would fire my husband. I needed the missionaries to think well of us in order to maintain the salary. So I covered up for him."[10]

This example bears out Lewis Codington's observation that local workers are sometimes more expensive, at least to agencies, than foreign missionaries, since they are often paid as employees who do not raise their own financial support. Codington also notes that while most of the people his agency works with are of high caliber, "Frequently we have found that people we thought were of high caliber and commitment have turned out to see the ministry as their job which puts food on their table."[11]

Missions by checkbook

Missions experts say that doing missions solely by checkbook has other perils. Money without accountability can kill initiative and create division and dependence overseas, just as misguided government spending does in the United States. Robertson McQuilkin created a stir with his 1999 article in *Christianity Today*, "Stop sending money! Breaking the cycle of missions dependency." In it, McQuilkin, a former missionary to Japan and former president of Columbia International University, stated, "Sharing financial resources in a way that is spiritually empowering and Great Commission-completing for both donor and recipient is our greatest unsolved problem."[12]

Even the well-intentioned giver faces subtle dangers. Roger Hedlund, a missionary with CBInternational in Madras, India, states, "Americans are especially vulnerable to an appeal that says, 'Give us your dollars, but not your sons and daughters.' If we do that, missionary vision will die within a generation, and the dollars will also (eventually) stop."[13] Lewis Codington agrees, saying, "I believe that one of my greatest contributions as a missionary is the privilege of challenging people back home in the US to become involved more in missions."[14]

Giving money only can also result in infrequent visits from missionaries, and given the crush of needs and ministries upon any church, a loss of commitment to global outreach is not just likely, it's a near certainty. Sending church members as missionaries helps to preclude this. Moreover those who wish only to give and not to go need to be reminded that if all ministry were done by Christians of the same ethnic groups as their non-Christian neighbors, some 4,000 sociolinguistic people groups without any Christian witness would remain unreached forever. The fact is, cross-cultural, Western missionaries will be needed for the foreseeable future. There is more than enough work for everyone.

Successes

Thankfully the non-Western missions movement, and the Western agencies that support and encourage it, is filled with top-notch servants of God, people whose faith sometimes puts pampered Westerners to shame. They represent not only the effectiveness of the Western missionary effort of the last two centuries, but the bulk of the missionary force of the 21st century.

To cite just one example, Isaac Anguyo was a city-living church youth leader and teacher in Uganda who had come from a very poor Islamic area that was frequently plagued by bandits. He was happily married, had four children, and worked in ministry. Anguyo was glad to leave the poverty and unrest of his childhood behind him. But after visiting friends in his hometown, Anguyo was shocked anew at the destitution he saw. In one home he was asked, "Isaac, have you come with a piece of soap?" He says now, "The church, which is supposed to be salt and light, was no longer able to perform its role."

Challenged at Billy Graham's 1986 conference for evangelists in Amsterdam, Anguyo began to formulate a plan. Today his plan has become a ministry called Here is Life, which trains church people in literacy, business techniques, and Muslim evangelism. More than 6,000 local people support the ministry through prayer and as volunteers.[15]

Such reputable and effective ministries deserve and need Western resources – and not always money. Technical know-how, training opportunities, and other services are sometimes far more helpful than cash. In fact, the highly effective Friends Missionary Prayer Band in India refuses to accept Western money for its ministries (although it will accept aid for capital improvements).

New roles?

Both raw need around the world and the biblical mandate to all Christians to spread the gospel everywhere ensure that Westerners will continue to have a job to do in world evangelization in the new millennium, but perhaps more as partners and less as leaders. Chuck Bennett, formerly of Partners International, says agencies should take a page from Hammer and Champy's 1993 business book, *Reengineering the Corporation:*

The fantastic growth and vitality of the church in the traditional mission fields makes it clear that it's time for Westerners to rethink their role and honestly ask themselves Hammer's and Champy's key question: Why do we do what we do at all? Pat answers like, "To spread the gospel," or "To reach the unreached," or, "To obey the Great Commission" will not do.... Perhaps a better way to phrase the question would be, Does what we do and the way we are now doing it still make a significant difference? If we brought half our missionaries home, would it really matter?[16]

FURTHER READING

"Stop sending money!" by Robertson McQuilkin, *Christianity Today*, 1 March 1999.

"The problem with success," by Chuck Bennett, *EMQ*, January 1996.

DISCUSSION QUESTIONS

1. *How much do the missionaries your church or agency supports cost per year?*

2. *Why are native missionaries said to be effective messengers of the gospel?*

3. *What are the pros and cons of financial support of native missionaries?*

4. *What could your church or agency do to avoid some of the pitfalls of financially supporting nationals?*

5. *What is the purpose of your church or organization?*

Chapter 3

Missionary Malaise

A couple came up to George Murray, then a missionary with TEAM, a large agency, at a missions conference to volunteer for overseas service. "God has spoken to us," they told Murray. "We both have our Bible training. We both believe that God wants us on the mission field. There's just one little thing that stands in our way. We just bought a home and we want to pay it off before we go."

"Well," said Murray, a former missionary to Italy, "how long will that take?"

"Twenty years," they replied.

That couple never made it to "the field." Instead, Murray said, "Everybody in their evangelical church is telling them how wise they were to build equity and to buy that house."[1]

For many prospective missionaries, the most daunting hurdle to overseas ministry is not learning a new language or taking two years of graduate-level Bible courses. It's not the possibility of culture shock, nor loneliness, nor even persecution. It's money. Often it's running the gauntlet of raising the needed funds from friends, neighbors, and churches, sometimes churches on the other side of the country. Sometimes it's giving up the salary and other perks that come with business careers.

One couple started the support-raising process with high hopes. Five grinding years later, however, they stood at only 75 percent of the amount needed. Reluctantly, they gave up on their vision and took on a more feasible ministry assignment.

Many missionaries are chronically undersupported. Some supporters, burdened by consumer debt, simply renege on their monthly pledges. Other, more faithful supporters die, and no one steps in to take up the slack. Missionaries will sometimes joke about how their predecessors were sent used tea bags, but the chuckling is tempered by the realization that they still usually receive only the leftovers from most churches.

This anecdotal evidence of what WEC International's Jim Raymo has aptly named "missionary malaise"[2] is supported by statistics. The typical church in the USA spends just 2 percent of its budget on local evangelism.[3] The picture for overseas efforts is mixed. The number of missionaries from North America who are serving at least one year overseas plunged from 50,500 in 1988 to just 40,143 in 1996,[4] before bouncing back somewhat to 42,996 in 1999.[5] The traditional week-long missionary conference has gone on the endangered species list.

Yet not everyone sees the glass as half empty. Paul McKaughan, executive director of the Evangelical Fellowship of Mission Agencies, says we simply can't know all that is going on because much of the new growth is coming from non-traditional quarters, such as the short-term movement (see chapter 10). "I am not sure there is as much of a 'missionary malaise' as there is a US mission movement that is flowing in new channels," he noted. "No one has any idea of the number of new agencies . . . that have been born in the last five to ten years. There is no idea of the number of people involved or the dollars involved in these movements."[6]

Unfortunately, this statement involves an unverifiable argument from silence. Meanwhile, the squeeze on resources for the traditional missions brokers is real. According to Empty Tomb, Inc., a religious nonprofit research organization, giving to mainline churches declined from 3.1 percent of members' after-tax income in 1968 to 2.6 percent in 1990. The Presbyterian Church (USA) was forced to slash its missions budget by 10 percent.[7] For 30 years Americans as a whole have never given more than 2.1 percent of their incomes.[8]

What about evangelicals, who are said to be more committed to the work of God? Despite all our talk about tithing, or giving 10 percent of our income to the church, the evangelical giving rate stands at 2.6 percent to charities of all kinds, not just to churches or missions agencies.[9] Some smaller missions boards have been forced to merge with larger ones in order to survive.

"I think there will have to be some kind of downsizing of the missions base here because the cost of supporting missionaries is exceeding the funds available," stated missionary statesman Jim Reapsome. "I think we'll see a tightening of the belt – it's already happening in some denominational agencies."[10]

Sources of the malaise

God and Mammon

In a booming, high tech-oriented economy in which personal incomes have reached a combined $8 trillion and the value of the US stock market has more than doubled in the last five years, giving to evangelical Protestant mission agencies has remained modest at best, at less than $3 billion annually. Yet there is some cause for hope. Giving for overseas ministries spiked upward by an impressive 21.8 percent between 1996 and 1998, at least partly tracking the incredible growth in financial wealth of many Americans during a bull market that reached from Wall Street to Main Street.[11] If financial markets continue to perform well as we enter the 21st century, missions agencies and other Great Commission initiatives can probably continue to expect to get at least a thin slice of the pie.

However, that less than $3 billion pales in comparison to the $76 billion given to religion across America in 1998. It looks even smaller when compared to the $107 billion managed in the Vanguard 500 Index, the largest stock mutual fund. It looks even punier when measured against the 4 billion people who don't even call themselves Christians across the world – less than 75 cents for every man, woman, and child who belongs to one of the world's non-Christian religions, or to no religion at all. Moreover, as pointed out by Ted Yamamori, president of the evangelical Food for the Hungry development organization, the giving is not distributed evenly. For all the current emphasis on unreached peoples, only .01 percent of the average Christian family income is aimed at reaching the so-called 10/40 Window,[12] an imaginary area with great spiritual and material need (see chapter 7).

Murray says the legitimate pursuit of financial equity is a pitfall. He's right. Even if we eschew conspicuous consumption as Christians (and not all of us manage to do even this), money can still be our god. The current passion for disciplined investing in mutual funds, the advantages of tax-deferred IRAs, day trading, and other financial strategies, as good as they may be, can be powerful disincentives to generous giving. Thanks to incessant media bombardment, we now know better the costs of *not* investing, and they are real. An initial investment of $10,000, earning an average of 12 percent annually, would become $930,510 in 40 years. That being so, the difficult decision to give money to missions becomes all the harder. Who in his right mind would give up the multiplicative power of compound interest? Viewed this way, every dollar given away instead of invested really is sacrificial, because of the cost to our future retirement, our kids' college education, or that small vacation home we've always dreamed about. A $10,000 gift can be seen as a million-dollar loss. (Of course, we are seeing only half the balance sheet right now, because the heavenly rewards for faithful giving can only be guessed at.)

Even when we are investing rather than spending, the consumer mindset can take over. Our treasure remains on earth, not in heaven, when we build our own balance sheets without investing in the kingdom, when we are always waiting for a better time to give, when our giving does not track our growing wealth, when we never even consider living below our means so that we can give more. Jesus, who said we are to lay up treasures in heaven and not on earth, stated that we cannot serve God and Mammon. These are hard issues in a wealthy society, even for well-meaning Christians. Murray's comment, however, bears thinking about: "My question is, if missionaries are willing to go without financial equity to get the gospel out, should we consider going without equity in order to help send them?"[13]

Indifference

Some overseas cross-cultural ministers work their standard four-year term hearing little or nothing from the churches that send them checks and little else. A care package, to them, is something college students, not missionaries, receive. When they return to the States at the end of their term (to raise more money), they are amazed at the opulence. They are largely unknown in the churches they visit, but it's easy to spot them: they are usually the ones whose clothing, and values, are just slightly out of date.

Those church people who do make an effort to talk to missionaries usually want to update them on the latest in fashion, in politics, in sports on this side of the ocean. Few ask intelligent, probing questions about issues missionaries face. Mirroring the superficiality in network news coverage of international events, few have an interest in what goes on in other parts of the world. Indeed, one church layman who is active in evangelizing his neighbors, business contacts, and coworkers is typical in his admission, "I just don't care what happens in other countries."

Unfortunately, some missions observers believe that attitude is common even among those studying for the ministry. Murray, president of Columbia International University in South Carolina and former general director of The Evangelical Alliance Mission, says only about 3,800 (about 5 percent) of the country's 70,000 graduating students in evangelical seminaries, Bible colleges, and similar institutions say they plan to become cross-cultural missionaries. The other 95 percent are planning to minister in North America – which is home to 5 percent of the world's people, and the best evangelized ones at that.[14]

Misperceptions

Some see the vast needs here and, forgetting the disparity of access to the gospel in different parts of the world, conclude that this country is just as much a mission field as India, Sudan, or China. "We're all missionaries" is the familiar, if grating, refrain. Yes, there are great needs in America, with people from nearly every country, religion, and ethnic group living here, but the disparity in access to the gospel is real. Yes, we do need to reach our own Jerusalems (Acts 1:8), but in so doing we dare not neglect all the Judeas, Samarias, and "uttermost parts."

Another problem is that "mission" budgets now include not only the traditional sending of people across oceans or cultures, but everything from neighborhood soup kitchens to the church building fund. But, as has been said before, if everything is mission, then nothing is mission.

Feeding the malaise is the creeping suspicion that America's day of world evangelization is over, that it's time to step back and let non-Westerners do it. (See chapter 2.) After all, there are more of them, they are more able to reach their own cultures, and, besides, the needs are pressing enough right here. While there is an element of truth in these assertions, the fact is, there are more than enough needs and challenges to keep every Christian busy for a lifetime. About 1.5 billion of the world's more than 6 billion people have never even heard the gospel.[15] By the year 2010, about 23 million children in the 15 sub-Saharan countries hardest hit by AIDS will have lost their mothers or both parents. Tens of thousands of people die annually in natural disasters. There is no lack of need – just a lack of will.

Self-centeredness

What's behind this? Jim Raymo, US candidate director for WEC International, lists a number of factors that have weakened North American commitment to missions in recent decades. First on his list is what he calls the "triumph of a self-centered lifestyle." He quotes sociologist Daniel Yankelovich as saying, "By concentrating day and night on your feelings, potentials, needs, wants and desires and by learning to assert them more freely, you do not become a freer, more spontaneous, more creative self; you become a narrower, more self-centered, more isolated one. You do not grow, you shrink."[16]

Another drag on missions commitment is family, and not without reason. The stresses of crossing cultures, presenting the gospel to non-Christians, and seemingly endless support-raising can be formidable enough for the single missionary. Throw in a family, and the obstacles to service can seem nearly impassable.[17] The Christian marketing subculture has responded. Christian bookstores have shelf after shelf of books on parenting, grand-parenting, strong-willed children, rekindling marital romance, homeschooling, and the like. Missions books, if they are available at all, are usually tucked safely away in hard-to-find crannies. One mail-order firm doesn't even give missions books a page in its catalogs anymore, though books on Christian counseling have multiplied, reflecting our fascination with the self. This fascination with self and family carries over to prospective missionaries.

"Perhaps as a response to recent Christian appeals for more concern for family relationships, prospective missionaries are asking more questions about provisions for their families," writes former missions professor Ted Ward in *Trinity World Forum*, the newsletter of the School of World Mission and Evangelism, Trinity Evangelical Divinity School. "No candidate should be faulted for a responsible attitude on matters of family welfare and solidarity, but dangers lie in the unbalanced presumption that all decisions about the future of one's children must be planned and contracted before bringing God's providence into the discussion. Old-timers in mission shake their heads in dismay."[18]

Speaking as a husband, a father, and a son, I must say that concern for family is good and right, but there are no guarantees of safety in the Christian life. Regrettably, some Christian families choose a safer and more prosperous path in the West because of a lack of faith. Since "we're all missionaries" anyway, one might as well keep family members from harm.

Raymo reminds us that what seems safest is not always God's best. He asks, "By overreacting fearfully on behalf of our families, are we not only missing the opportunity to achieve something for God cross-culturally, but also potentially depriving our families of a wonderfully stretching and enriching experience?"[19]

The remedy

A vision of God

Echoing John F. Kennedy, we should ask not what the kingdom can do for us, but what we can do for the kingdom. We should not, however, take the missions option simply because of the great needs of the world and the lostness of mankind apart from saving faith in Christ. Merely responding to needs, while noble, is a sure path to burnout. Jesus rightly said, "You will always have the poor among you." The needs are overwhelming, and always will be. We must be *called* to missions. Only a clear and compelling vision of God can motivate us in the face of increasingly stiff cultural winds.

William Carey, who has been called "the father of modern missions," had to struggle against similar winds. He was a poor Baptist shoemaker and pastor whose wife, Dorothy, had little interest in anything beyond their small English village. When one day Carey suggested to a group of pastors that they had a responsibility to take the gospel to the pagans in other lands, John Ryland, Sr., a learned and well-respected man, shot back, "Young man, sit down. When God pleases to convert the heathen, he will do it without your aid or mine."[20]

Undeterred, the humble Carey pressed on. Using his own hand-made globe of the world and the limited reference works available to him, Carey wrote a compelling document that basically sparked the current Protestant missions enterprise: *An Enquiry into the Obligations of Christians to Use Means for the Conversion of the Heathens*. Carey used many means in four decades of difficult ministry in India. In his diary he wrote, "I feel that it is good to commit my soul, my body, and my all, into the hands of God. Then the world appears little, the promises great, and God an all-sufficient portion." His motto remains an inspiration: "Expect great things from God, attempt great things for God."[21]

God at the center

Perhaps the reason many of today's churches are so careless about missions is because their view of God differs so drastically from Carey's. His God was the sovereign Lord of the universe, who expected his people to fulfill his command to disciple the nations and whose purposes cannot be thwarted.

Sometimes it seems our current strategizing and promotion tend to put people, rather than God, at the center of the missions process. We call people "resistant" or "receptive" to the gospel, as if God has no say over the human will, as if it is our job alone to "soften them up" so that the Spirit can work. Some of the current prayer emphases (see chapter 9) imply that God is reluctant or weak and must be roused to save people. As one evangelical professor has remarked sarcastically, it seems that "if we just pray hard enough, God will do more to save people." Or we latch onto evangelistic strategies that seem to be working, as if the power of regenerating the human heart lies in the method rather than in the God who orchestrates all the conditions that contribute to making people "open" or "closed" to the gospel.

Given these attitudes in the churches, is it any wonder that there is a lack of missionary motivation? If God is dependent on us to finish his work, how can we really be sure it will ultimately get done? Is such a "God" worth all the bother?

Scripture's view

The cure for missionary malaise will not come in a new marketing strategy, but in a new look at Scripture, for it is there that we see God clearly. While the Bible, from Genesis to Revelation, is filled with powerful missionary texts that can inspire God's people to get serious about missions, I would like to look briefly at two from Acts, which chronicles the explosive growth of the church against all odds. Each deserves a full exegesis and sermon, but this glimpse should give us at least a hint of the awesome God of missions.

In Acts 4 Peter and John are brought before the hostile Jewish leaders in Jerusalem to explain how they had healed a man who had been lame since birth. Peter, who weeks before had denied his faith under the questioning of a servant girl, rooted their actions in the will of a sovereign God. Peter boldly declared, "It is by the name of Jesus Christ of Nazareth, whom you crucified but whom God raised from the dead, that this man stands before you healed. . . . Salvation is found in no one else, for there is no other name under heaven given to men by which we must be saved."

After Peter and John were released, they held a church prayer meeting, asking God for courage, and reminding themselves and God that the collusion of Jew and Gentile against Jesus was "what (God's) power and will had decided beforehand should happen. Now, Lord, consider their threats and enable your servants to speak your word with great boldness," they prayed. "Stretch out your hand to perform miraculous signs and wonders through the name of your holy servant Jesus."

Luke, the writer of Acts, records what happened next: "After they prayed, the place where they were meeting was shaken. And they were all filled with the Holy Spirit and spoke the word of God boldly."

Acts 17 describes the apostle Paul's great distress on finding that the streets of the great pagan metropolis of Athens were "full of altars to false gods." One altar was even dedicated "To an Unknown God," and Paul refers to this altar when preaching the gospel to a group of haughty philosophers at the Areopagus.

"Now what you worship as something unknown I am going to proclaim to you," he said audaciously. Citing their poets, Paul presented the Lord as the sovereign Creator and Ruler of the world, near every person. "In the past God overlooked such ignorance, but now he commands all people everywhere to repent. For he has set a day when he will judge the world with justice by the man he has appointed. He has given proof of this by raising him from the dead."

There is no reason for malaise. A day of judgment has been set and is more certain than yesterday's headlines. God is orchestrating all events and peoples to bring himself glory. He calls us to join him in the awesome task, expecting great things from him and attempting great things for him.

FURTHER READING

"Reflections on missionary malaise," by Jim Raymo, *EMQ*, October 1997, pp. 442–6.

"The right stuff," by Deann Alford, *World Pulse*, 21 August 1998.

Mission Handbook, John A. Siewert and Edna G. Valdez, editors (Monrovia: MARC, 1997).

"The faithful witness of William Carey," by Timothy George, *EMQ*, October 1992.

DISCUSSION QUESTIONS

1. *Do you see what this chapter has labeled missionary malaise in your church? In what ways?*

2. *How important are your money and your family to you? Do you find them a hindrance or a help in your missions involvement?*

3. *How does our view of God shape our commitment to and zeal for the missions task?*

4. *What steps can you take to deepen your own passion for spreading the glory of Christ?*

Chapter 4

Missionary Care

In 1793, a year after the publication of his groundbreaking pamphlet *An Enquiry into the Obligation of Christians to Use Means for the Conversion of the Heathens*, William Carey was primed to go to India. Carey, who would come to be known as the father of modern missions, had taken personal responsibility to do his part in reaching India for Christ. He was to accompany a surgeon, John Thomas, who had worked previously for the East India Company. There was just one problem: Carey's wife, Dorothy, refused to go.

Eight months pregnant and with a four-year-old son, Peter, Dorothy wanted no part of leaving England for the Hindu heartland. A biographer says she was "impervious" to her husband's pleadings; only Thomas's "dire predictions of the consequences" changed her mind – and the promise that her sister Catharine could accompany her. A six-week delay in the departure also helped, for by then she had given birth to another son, Jabez.

The five-month journey did little to brighten Mrs Carey's spirits, and the family's arrival on 11 November 1793 marked the start of six years of hardship. The Careys moved from place to place, seeking to establish a mission station. They suffered from all sorts of illnesses, including dysentery and malaria. Catharine's decision to accept a marriage proposal and return to England six months after their arrival was a critical blow.

The stresses of childbirth (Dorothy had borne William six children in England, two of whom had died as toddlers) and raising a family far from what she considered home no doubt also took their toll. Perhaps the *coup de grâce* for Dorothy, however, was the death of Peter in 1794.

Soon after the birth of the Careys' seventh child, in 1798, Dorothy began having delusions. While the family finally settled in at the mission station in Serampore in 1800, from which William did some of his greatest work, for Dorothy it was too late. Sorrowfully, in 1801 William Carey wrote to his sisters, "Mrs Carey is obliged to be constantly confined; she has long gotten worse and worse, but fear both of my own life and hers, and the desire of the police of the place, obliged me to agree to her confinement."

Six years later, on 8 December 1807, Dorothy Carey died at the age of 52.[1]

Troubling questions

Such an account is disturbing, not only for the personal tragedy it highlights, but for the troubling questions it raises for people committed to making Christ known among the nations. We all believe that God had a plan in raising up William Carey, a poor, humble and devout shoemaker, to turn the church and the world of missions upside down. But we struggle when we consider Dorothy. What was God's plan for her? As H. Miriam Ross asked in her article for *Evangelical Missions Quarterly*, "What about Dorothy?"

These questions are not just academic; they relate to our own involvement in missions, too. Were Dorothy's dementia and death an acceptable price to pay for the launch of the modern Protestant missions movement? What, if anything, could have been done differently so that Dorothy could have shared in the ministry and been a help, and not a hindrance, to her husband? What price are we willing to pay in advancing the cause of Christ? What level of suffering – in culture shock, additional health problems, increased safety risks, bickering with fellow missionaries, and so on – are we willing to accept as part of God's plan for our involvement in world missions? What level of responsibility are we willing to take to alleviate or eliminate some of these problems?

Scope of the problem

Missionary service has always been a demanding calling in Christ's kingdom. The gospel itself, even when told and demonstrated with love and humility, causes offense. While God has prepared some people to respond immediately to the free offer of salvation with joy, most times the response is somewhere on the continuum between hostility and indifference.

One day Johan Lukasse, the president of the Belgian Evangelical Mission, was out sharing the good news in his native Belgium, an affluent and highly secular country. One man responded to Lukasse's approach with a brusque: "Mister, what do you need?" As Lukasse groped for a response, the man added, "Tell me what you need, and I'll buy it for you."[2] He took Lukasse for a beggar. Such reactions can wear on the self-esteem of the best of missionaries, even in comfortable surroundings.

In harsh ones, the stresses of living in an unforgiving and unfamiliar culture can, as they did for Dorothy, become too much to bear. While much has been made of US missionary dropouts, the problem is worldwide. The non-Western missions movement is much better known for sending people out than for keeping them on the field. During the Brazilian National Missions Congress in October 1993, participants were stunned to hear that of the 5,400 missionaries sent out in the previous five years, the vast majority had returned within a year. Worse, about 90 percent of the returnees did not go back. A Colombian missions leader has estimated that 40 percent of all Latin American missionaries return from their assignments early and discouraged because of a lack of training, a lack of on-field pastoral support, and a lack of finances.[3]

Seeking to get a handle on the problem, the Missions Commission of the World Evangelical Fellowship commissioned a study of evangelical missionaries from 14 countries. The findings, published in the book *Too Valuable to Lose: Exploring the Cases and Cures of Missionary Attrition*, estimated that an average of 5.1 percent of the missions force leaves the field annually for preventable reasons.[4]

Attrition is not just a missionary problem. Businesses sending workers overseas in today's global economy are finding increasing reluctance on the part of their employees to work in other countries. Over 80 percent of firms in a recent survey reported that workers had recently refused overseas assignments, citing dual-career issues or family issues. Accordingly, more and more companies are focusing on helping their workers adjust to the stresses and challenges of overseas living. Another option is what is called the "virtual expatriate," someone who uses e-mail, cell phones, and other modern tools to keep tabs on a foreign assignment without actually living there. While such options can be made to work, they are not always ideal. A management researcher told the *Wall Street Journal*, "Nothing can replace face-to-face communication." How much more so in the missions world.[5]

Rugged individualists?

Missionaries have the reputation of being rugged individualists. The stereotype has been that all you have to do with missionaries is give them their marching orders, point them in the right direction, and send them off to their ministries, where they will stay for 30 or 40 years (excluding furloughs) until the job is done. The reality is far different. Jim Reapsome notes that some of the most effective missionary communicators with home churches are those who admit their vulnerability and pain, who are honest about their personal and spiritual struggles. Such people give hope to people in the pews who struggle, as well as providing realistic role models.[6]

Wycliffe Bible Translators and its sister agency, the Summer Institute of Linguistics, have begun changing their view of what a missionary is. They have started a new "Member Care" division within the agencies. Their in-house newsletter, *InterCom*, noted that translators have been expected to be among the most rugged and resourceful of missionary recruits. An article stated, "We evaluate all recruits to see if they are what we call hardy personalities. We expect that we'll be able to do a lot for ourselves and think twice before bothering someone with our problems. Somewhat reluctantly, we acknowledge that counseling is not a shameful thing. Underneath, however, we may think that we just need to pray more and learn our Bibles better. The reality is, however, that at some time or another we will all need help beyond our resources."[7]

Services rendered

Agencies used to do little for the Dorothy Careys of the missions world. Perhaps the missionaries of the past were, as older missionaries are sometimes heard to mutter, a hardier lot than today's adult children of alcoholics, products of broken homes, and consumers of psychological counseling. Today's cross-cultural workers, instead of carrying their coffins with them to the field as their predecessors did to West Africa, carry their laptop PCs. Instead of sending their kids off to boarding school, they inquire about every educational option available on the field, from home schooling to national schools. There are many agencies to choose from, and missionary care issues play an increasing role in which agencies workers decide to go with.

Agencies, as in so many other areas, are being forced to respond. Thankfully, more and more are doing it willingly, believing that there is no reason to have one more Dorothy Carey than is absolutely necessary. Besides Wycliffe/SIL, other agencies are making a commitment to what is now called "member care." The International Mission Board of the Southern Baptist Convention provides a range of services before a missionary's appointment, on the field, during furlough, and upon retirement. The Evangelical Alliance Mission debriefs workers on furloughs "to review and assist with family, emotional, and reentry issues."

TEAM, along with many larger agencies, also provides medical insurance and a retirement plan.[8]

Specialized agencies to help missionaries with their personal and family needs have also sprung up. The Link Care Center in Fresno, California, provides counseling to missionaries on home assignment and on the field, to enhance their effectiveness and keep them working productively. To aid missionaries on the field who are caught in crises ranging from rape to war, several agencies support a new ministry called the Mobile Member Care Team.[9] One agency, Crisis Consulting International, Ventura, California, helps agencies negotiate for the release of workers taken captive or held as hostages. One New York-based agency, Interaction, provides expertise on the needs of the children of missionaries, as well as other missionary care issues. The "missionary kid" movement is coming of age. The first International Conference on Missionary Kids was held at the Faith Academy boarding school in Manila in 1984. Regional events are now convened regularly for workers in Asia, Europe, Africa, and the Americas. A recent conference in Kandern, Germany, attracted more than 400 delegates.[10]

Drawbacks

Yet, as with anything, there are drawbacks. There is the matter of cost. Missionary costs are as high as they are in part because of care issues. Helping missionaries with their problems costs money. Looking at it one way, every dollar not committed to missionary care is a dollar that can be invested in ministry. But it can and should also be viewed the other way, too. Every dollar invested in helping missionaries stay on the field keeps their ministries healthy and productive.

Resources devoted to caring for missionaries can also drive a wedge between them and the people they work with. Tom Steller, missions pastor of Bethlehem Baptist Church, admits that "the care we give our missionaries also puts them at times in an awkward situation among the nationals with whom they work.

They have finances, a passport, easy access to a plane ticket out, medical care, and so on. These set them apart from the people they have come to serve."[11] One suggestion by Brent Lindquist of the Link Care Center is, whenever possible, to get help on the field where one serves.[12]

Another pitfall is that the emphasis on member care may tempt missionaries to ask what their agencies can do for them, rather than what they can do for their agencies. While care issues need not undercut the role of missionary sacrifice in obeying the Great Commission, that is a danger. In the eyes of their older colleagues, some recruits concentrate much more on family issues than is seemly.

Conclusion

Churches and missionaries, for the most part, appreciate this new emphasis on member care. Alluding to 3 John, Steller notes, "To send in a manner worthy of God includes doing 'whatever' for the brethren going out for the sake of his name. ... The Golden Rule is a powerful force for caring for our missionaries."[13]

It's safe to say that Dorothy Carey would approve.

FURTHER READING

"What about Dorothy?" by H. Miriam Ross, *EMQ*, October 1992.

"My child in the national school," by Cynthia Storrs, *EMQ*, April 1999.

"The increasing scope of 'member care'," by Kelly and Michèle O'Donnell, *EMQ*, October 1990.

"Crisis intervention for missionaries," by Karen Carr, *EMQ*, October 1997.

"Maturing 'missionary kid' movement is coming of age," by Janet Blomberg and Joyce Bowers, *World Pulse*, 15 May 1998.

"The 'CACTUS Kit' for building resilient teams," by Kelly O'Donnell, *EMQ*, January 1999.

Missionary Care: Counting the Cost for World Evangelization, by Kelly O'Donnell (Pasadena: William Carey Library, 1992).

Raising Resilient MKs, edited by Joyce M. Bowers (Colorado Springs: Mission Training International, 1998).

DISCUSSION QUESTIONS

1. *How much suffering should accompany missionary ministry?*

2. *What are some of the pluses and minuses of the new missionary care emphasis?*

3. *What sacrifices are you willing to face to do your part in the Great Commission?*

4. *What steps does your church or ministry take to make sure that missionaries are properly cared for?*

Chapter 5

Theological Drift

By today's standards, J. Hudson Taylor was an extremist. To prepare himself for expected missionary hardships in China, this 19th-century Englishman subsisted on a loaf of bread and a pound of apples each day, seriously undercutting his own frail health. Once in China, he was drawn to the interior, where hardships were many and Christians were few. In an attempt to remove Western cultural impediments, Taylor donned Chinese dress and died his sandy hair black and pulled it together in a Chinese pigtail, prompting rebukes and derision from other missionaries. Yet at its zenith, the organization Taylor founded, the China Inland Mission, had more than 1,300 missionaries at one time in China, 6,000 in all, laying the foundation for the explosive growth of the church there today.

What drove him on, through discouragement and depression? In part, of course, his love for and obedience to Jesus. But another focus was the plight of the millions of Chinese people who had never heard the gospel and were doomed to hell unless someone told them. "Souls on every hand are perishing for lack of knowledge; more than 1,000 every hour are passing away into death and darkness," Taylor said.[1]

This vision was not Taylor's alone. Missionary Robert Moffat motivated David Livingstone, the great missionary to Africa, by saying he had "sometimes seen, in the morning sun, the smoke of a thousand villages where no missionary had ever been."[2]

John Orme, executive director of the Interdenominational Foreign Mission Association, says all the great missionary pioneers in the last 200 years have been motivated by belief in hell. "William Carey, Hudson Taylor, and the founders of every mission in the IFMA shared a common conviction that personal faith in Jesus Christ is the only way of salvation for all people everywhere and that those who die without this saving knowledge face eternal damnation."[3]

Jonathan Edwards, perhaps America's premier theologian, used widespread belief in hell to great effect. His classic sermon "Sinners in the Hands of an Angry God" played no small part in bringing people to repentance during the pre-Revolutionary Great Awakening.

Hell and the unevangelized

This belief used to be an integral part of the faith of all who called themselves Christians. Today, increasing numbers in the Bible-believing camp hold out the possibility of a salvation that encompasses a much wider set of people, a proposition first advanced by theological liberals such as John Sanders, Paul Knitter, and John Hick.[4] Evangelical theologians such as John Stott,[5] J.N.D. Anderson,[6] and Gregory Boyd[7] are among those who have called into question traditional evangelical doctrines about hell and the fate of the unevangelized.

Stott himself is one of the most prominent evangelical theologians allowing for the possibility that the unsaved will not suffer conscious, eternal torment in hell, but will at some point be annihilated. J.I. Packer is cognizant of the amazing theological drift on this and related issues. "At one time, evangelical Protestants stoutly maintained the unending agony of those who leave this world without Christ against all suggestions of universal salvation or the post-mortem anni-hilation of the godless, and they enforced the missionary imperative," Packer writes in the foreword to Ajith Fernando's important book, *Crucial Questions About Hell*. "Today, however, universalism, the doctrine of a finally empty hell, is rampant, and so are theories of salvation through non-Christian religions and of unbelievers being finally snuffed out. . . . Emphasis on the lostness of the lost has come to be almost taboo. The shift is startling."[8]

Asked about current trends in missions, Jim Reapsome, former editor of *Evangelical Missions Quarterly* and *World Pulse*, stated, "Probably the most scary thing is that our theological foundations are eroding. There's not a clear-cut line between the saved and the lost. Pluralism in America, multiculturalism, all this meshes together so that everybody will be saved some way or another."[9]

In his groundbreaking 1987 study of the beliefs of American evangelical college students and seminarians, *Evangelicalism: The Coming Generation*, James Davison Hunter said that a third of those polled held out some possibility of salvation for those who had never heard.[10] These were not undiscerning pew-sitters; they were the church's future leaders. Many of these young people, no doubt, now hold prominent positions in Christian ministry. Theologian Ronald Nash, in his 1994 book *Is Jesus the Only Savior?*, estimates that more than half of the evangelical leaders in denominational or missions leadership and of missions professors at evangelical colleges and seminaries may believe that people can be saved by Christ without specifically turning to him for forgiveness of their sins.[11]

According to a recent Gallup poll, such views are now widespread. Some 52 percent of American adults believe that all good people will go to heaven, regardless of their beliefs. Even 45 percent of those Americans classified as born-again Christians say a person can earn a place in heaven through good works. Seven percent believe that because God loves all people, he will not let them perish.[12]

Historical background

Where did this mindset come from? Feelings of compassion, perhaps, but not from the Bible. The so-called higher criticism of the 19th century, of course, undermined confidence in the written Word of God. The surprising strength and resiliency of the world's other great religions was another factor. Many Christians at the dawn of the 20th century believed these religious systems were dying, and that the 20th century would be a "Christian century." But they were wrong.

The appearance of Hindu guru Swami Vivekananda at Chicago's World's Fair in 1893 is generally seen as the genesis of the modern push for pluralism, the belief that all religions teach basically the same thing, that all beliefs, if sincerely held, lead to God, and that people can be saved through their own religions. Such thinking spawned the 1993 Parliament of the World's Religions, attended in Chicago by prominent religious figures from around the world. Some 6,000 people attended a follow-up Parliament in Cape Town in December 1999. Meanwhile, Vatican II, the 1960s restatement of Catholic doctrine, opened the door to inclusivism, the belief that people can be saved by Christ and his death, but without specifically turning to him in faith.[13] Inclusivists sometimes distinguish between "Christians," those who have consciously turned to Christ in faith, and "believers," those who trust in God's mercy and grace without specifically turning to Christ.[14]

Collapsing consensus

The pressure to soften the exclusive claims of Christ and the finality of hell is intense. Society is increasingly multicultural. In today's postmodern era, the Christian consensus has collapsed, which is why un-Christian positions on homosexual marriage and the right to abortion have become so pervasive. Christians now work and live alongside Muslims, Buddhists, and Hindus, many of whom seem more moral than they. Compassion and a desire to tolerate differences and get along have encouraged many evangelicals to dilute troubling biblical doctrines on lostness and hell. Claims of religious truth are often seen not as universally true but as expressions of personal preference, to take or leave as one chooses.

Hunter writes, "Intensive cultural pluralism, one of the hallmarks of the modern world order, has, at least in the United States, institutionalized an ethic of toleration and civility."[15] The weight of that ethic can be heavy on those who dare challenge it. Chapter 20 gives examples of how recent attempts to assert and act upon traditional Christian doctrines have been met with ritualized outrage from offended groups. The Southern Baptists, in particular, have been lightning rods because of their size and their commitment to unashamedly stand for the gospel against the cultural tide. In 1999 they prompted cries of intolerance when they issued members with booklets on how to pray for Jews and Hindus. In a letter to the *Wall Street Journal,* two Jewish activists asserted that "Southern Baptists are, unwittingly or not, sowing seeds of contempt. The implication is clear; the prayers of Jews are misguided and incomplete. . . . There are many religious denominations that have learned that like the stars in heaven, we all bring light to God's universe. Others continue to insist they alone illuminate the world."[16]

A Southern Baptist plan to bring 100,000 missionaries to Chicago in the summer of 2000 prompted cries from area clergy for the evangelists *not* to come. A letter sent by the Council of Religious Leaders of Metropolitan Chicago warned that the proposed campaign could contribute to an atmosphere encouraging hate crimes. "I'm always fearful when we in the Christian community move from the rightful claim that Jesus is decisive for us, to the presupposition that non-Christians . . . are outside of God's plan of salvation," stated Bishop C. Joseph Sprague of the United Methodist Church's Northern Illinois Conference. "That smacks of a kind of non-Jesus-like arrogance."[17]

Biblical considerations

One wonders what Bible such critics are reading. While the suggestions for further reading at the end of this chapter will provide a wealth of insight on the subject, I must say that even a cursory reading of the Bible supports an exclusive gospel. In a display of what non-Christians have called arrogance – or blasphemy – Jesus said that he was the way and the truth and the life, and that no one comes to the Father except through him (John 14:6). Right after speaking of God's love for the world being manifested in sending his only Son (John 3:16), the Lord added that anyone who does not believe in him stands condemned (3:18). The Apostle Peter said that there is no name other than Jesus by which people must be saved (Acts 4:12). Paul said only those who believe in Jesus can be saved (Rom. 10:12–15).

The Bible is also very clear about the eternal duration and conscious torments of hell (Isa. 66:24; Luke 16:19–31; Matt. 25:46; Rev. 20:10). The Bible also makes it clear that the reality of hell and the fear of punishment are proper motivations for both the missionary effort and for turning to Christ in faith (Jonah 3:4–10; Acts 2:40; 2 Cor. 5:11; Luke 12:5; Acts 17:30–31).

The desire to find an escape clause from hell for people who, it is often said, "through no fault of their own," do not believe in Christ shortchanges both the seriousness of sin and the holiness of God. Perhaps we find it difficult to believe in hell because we find it difficult to believe in our own sin. The gospel has always been a good news–bad news proposition. As Paul said, "For the message of the cross is foolishness to those who are perishing, but to us who are being saved it is the power of God" (1 Cor. 1:18).

What next?

In the search to find ways other than the negative imagery of hell to motivate postmodern Christians, there is a new focus in churches on the positive aspects of faith and missionary obedience. It is possible that fixating on the fate of the lost moves the focus too much from God to people, and is inadequate as a lasting motive. Unfortunately, however, much of the current language of the church is still too people-centered, focusing on the temporal benefits of knowing Christ, such as the peace and purpose (and sometimes the prosperity) he provides. John Piper suggests, helpfully, that we need to be thinking about the glory of God: "Missions is not the ultimate goal of the church. Worship is. Missions exists because worship doesn't. Worship is ultimate, not missions, because God is ultimate, not man. When this age is over, and the countless millions of the redeemed fall on their faces before the throne of God, missions will be no more. It is a temporary necessity. But worship abides forever."[18]

Still, there is no getting around the dark side of the good news if one is to be faithful to Scripture. That so many have done so shows how far off the path we have come. Robertson McQuilkin, former president of the missions-minded Columbia International University, believes the shift has been profound even among evangelicals since the 1974 Lausanne Congress on World Evangelization: "The most critical issue for missions in the 21st century is theological. . . . Are those who have never heard of Christ's saving grace certainly lost? If there is any question about this, the heroic sacrifices of missionaries in the 19th and 20th centuries will not be forthcoming in the 21st. The surprise is that few would have thought, in 1974, that such would become a major theological issue among those calling themselves evangelical."[19]

Orme concurs. "Today the wider-hope theory has begun to creep insidiously into our own evangelical circles; the theological tensions which this creates are felt by us all. . . . Supporters, candidates, staffs, and missionaries are being affected by this dangerous influence."[20]

No research has been done to prove a link between evangelical theological drift and declining missionary interest, but drift is almost certainly a key factor in the church's missionary malaise (see chapter 3). Overseas Christians who are traveling to the West or consuming our books are also having to deal with drift. Christians in Sri Lanka and India, religious minorities themselves, are also under strong pressure to succumb to pluralism. Will any more Hudson Taylors be created in this climate? Jim Raymo of WEC International, writing in *Evangelical Missions Quarterly*, puts the matter succinctly: "If the unsaved do not face judgment and unending agony – the historic Christian position – then why risk life, limb, and career to reach them?"[21]

FURTHER READING

Crucial Questions About Hell, by Ajith Fernando (Wheaton: Crossway, 1994).

The Evangelical Left, by Millard Erickson (Grand Rapids: Baker, 1997).

Through No Fault of Their Own?, edited by William V. Crockett and James G. Sigountos (Grand Rapids: Baker, 1991).

Christianity and Comparative Religion, by J.N.D. Anderson (Downers Grove: InterVarsity Press, 1977).

Evangelical Review of Theology, January 1991.

Christianity and the Religions: A Biblical Theology of World Religions, by Edward Rommen and Harold Netland (Pasadena: William Carey Library, 1995).

More Than One Way? Four Views on Salvation in a Pluralistic World, edited by Dennis L. Okholm and Timothy R. Phillips (Grand Rapids: Zondervan, 1995).

Evangelicalism: The Coming Generation, by James Davison Hunter (Chicago and London: The University of Chicago Press, 1987).

"Hell hath no fury," by Jeffery L. Sheler, *US News & World Report*, 31 January 2000.

Two Views of Hell: A Biblical and Theological Dialogue, by Edward William Fudge and Robert A. Peterson (Downers Grove: InterVarsity Press, 2000).

DISCUSSION QUESTIONS

1. *Will the unevangelized face an eternity of conscious punishment in hell? Give biblical reasons for your answer.*

2. *Is there a link between what one believes about the lost and one's missionary motivation?*

3. *What might be some ways to sensitively communicate this truth to Christians and non-Christians?*

4. *How should Christians respond when the world challenges traditional evangelical beliefs?*

Chapter 6

Women in Missions

It was February 1991. Jeanine Brabon, an OMS International missionary and a professor of Old Testament at the Biblical Seminary of Colombia, Medellin, had heard of a revival among the assassins and terrorists in Medellin's notorious Bellavista National Jail. This was the facility where inmates had played soccer with a human skull. A former inmate, Oscar Osorio, had been changed by Jesus Christ, and he invited Brabon to come see the revival there firsthand. Intrigued, but not sure what lay ahead, Brabon accepted.

Osorio, now the prison chaplain, met her downtown and drove her to Bellavista (which means "beautiful view"). On the way, he asked her to preach to the inmates. "Who, uh, is my audience?" she asked. "*Sicarios* and terrorists," he replied. (In Colombia's drug-warped society, a *sicario* is a hired gun.)

"Okay," Brabon said, "I'll do it."

When the two arrived, Brabon, the object of curiosity from the guards, had to undergo the customary body search and fingerprinting. Soon it was over, though, and they entered the locked area where the inmates lived. Immediately the smell of human waste, body odor, and rotten food assaulted them.

Fighting her fear, Brabon preached on God's mercy and then sat down. As she watched, 23 of the inmates, their formerly hardened faces drenched with tears, came forward to pray for salvation.[1]

Brabon was instrumental in applying her academic expertise in the founding of the Bellavista Bible Institute, a seminary behind prison walls from which scores have graduated.[2]

Role expectations

Women have always been the backbone of the missionary effort. Mary Slessor in Nigeria, Rosalind Goforth in India, Gladys Aylward in China, Helen Roseveare in the Congo, Rachel Saint in Ecuador, Betty Stam in China, Lilias Trotter with Muslims, and Joy Ridderhof with Gospel Recordings are just the better-known women who have served in God's world outreach. Countless others have served just as faithfully, but less conspicuously. Women will continue providing their incalculable contributions in the third millennium, just as they did in the first two. However, the expectations of their roles are changing, thanks in no small part to the feminist movement that began in the USA in the 1960s.

The evangelical church, consciously or not, has never been immune to cultural influences. Missions does not occur in a vacuum. Attitudes toward wealth, poverty, religious pluralism, even homosexuality, have all been affected by the thinking of the larger society. Christians have been forced to reexamine their beliefs and what Scripture really teaches in light of these powerful cultural influences. Women's roles are no different.

As always, there is good and bad news here. In the secular arena, the feminist movement has brought women remarkable gains that even the most conservative evangelicals would be hard-pressed to deny, including better pay, less discrimination, and more opportunities. However, the revolution brought about by the Betty Friedans, Gloria Steinems, and Bella Abzugs of this world has also brought us more sexual promiscuity, more divorce, and more day care.

In years past, most women in the United States aspired to the traditional roles of wife, mother, and homemaker. Now many women, if they still seek these roles, want them in addition to professional goals, which in years past were the province of men. Talk of a "glass ceiling" for women has filtered down from the business world to the missions world. While little is heard about a glass ceiling *per se* in missions, there is much talk about exercising one's spiritual gifts or being allowed to respond to God's call.

Despite the historical examples of the women listed above and the biblical record of women like Priscilla, Lydia, Euodia, and Syntyche – missions has been mostly a male province, at least when it comes to decision making. And, with a few exceptions, it still is. Of the member agencies of the Interdenominational Foreign Mission Association, for example, not one has a female CEO,[3] even though 53.5 percent of the IFMA missionaries from the USA (and 55.7 percent from Canada) are women.[4] The IFMA does, however, have a female president – Susan Perlman, an executive with the San Francisco-based Jews for Jesus.

At a missions conference several years ago, Jim Reapsome and eight other leaders in missions fielded "the toughest questions you can imagine" from churchgoers. On the last day, someone got up and asked, "Why are there no women on the panel? Women do make up two-thirds of the missionary force." Reapsome said later, "We felt as if we had been caught with our hands in the cookie jar."[5]

Such questions are being asked more and more frequently. As Laurel Cocks, formerly the coordinator of workshops for women missionaries with Greater Europe Mission, has observed, "Interest in issues of women in missions has waxed and waned over the years. Now I am observing another wave of interest in women's issues – even a ground swell."[6]

Gary Corwin, the editor of *Evangelical Missions Quarterly*, participated in a study group examining the history of women in missions in which some of these issues were aired: "For the first time I was part of a meeting in which several talented and capable women spoke poignantly to the issues of women in missions without feminist stridency on the one hand, or passive, if sometimes unenthusiastic, acceptance of the status quo on the other. . . . This group made itself vulnerable through transparency, frequently revealing pain without bitterness."[7]

Perlman speaks as a decision-making leader in her organization, with significant experience designing national ad campaigns and working with other professionals in major media outlets. Women, she said, "sometimes have to meet a higher standard than their male counterparts to be considered for such positions. Or, they tend to have to prove themselves over a longer trial period. It's not all that different than what it takes for women in any profession that has traditionally been male-dominated to find acceptance."[8]

Karen Carr, a psychologist who founded a ministry to help missionaries facing crisis situations, states: "My experience as a woman leading workshops within the evangelical missions community has been that there is a small minority of men who are not open to the leadership of women. I've had several who have said that in the beginning of the workshop they were skeptical that they could learn anything from a woman, but by the end . . . they had changed their minds."[9]

There are several reasons for the skepticism. Perlman, as one who out of conviction admits no gender barriers to leadership, puts them in a nutshell: "The barriers that are there are, sadly, ones of either holding to convention, of insecurity of those who hold power in existing structures, or of those who, while sincere, have a faulty understanding of Scripture."[10]

Oh yes, Scripture – the elephant in the living room of the debate.

Grappling with the Bible

While God's Word has not changed, interpretations of its meaning sometimes do. This includes the touchy subject of women's roles. But evangelicals, who are heirs of the Protestant Reformation, are not allowed to simply disregard what the Bible says when it goes out of fashion in the larger culture. As Clark Pinnock noted in his classic book, *Biblical Revelation*, "Scripture is a gift of God for the good of his church and gospel, a gift well suited to the needs of sinful man."[11]

To some extent, however, new understandings of the text are inevitable, even healthy. William Carey, for example, battled hard against the entrenched hyper-Calvinism of his day that saw the Great Commission as given only to the apostles. Yet time-honored interpretations of the Bible have been around for a reason and deserve at least the benefit of the doubt. This includes the traditional view of women's roles.

While this is not the place for an extended discussion on what the Bible says on the subject, a summary of the two basic positions will help to put the missions angle in sharper focus, allowing readers to look at other sources and make up their own minds (if they haven't already).

The traditional view, sometimes called complementarianism, holds that men and women, both made in the image of God, are equal in dignity and worth (Gen. 1:27). Yet they have different, interdependent, and complementary roles (1 Cor. 11:11–12). The man is, generally, the head of the woman (1 Cor. 11:7–9), called to lead, while the woman is to be his helper (Gen. 2:20). In Christian marriage, wives are to submit to their husbands, as the church does to Christ (Eph. 5:22–24, 1 Pet. 3:1–2), while husbands are to love their wives, giving up their lives for their wives to help in their sanctification (Eph. 5:25–31). In the church, women and men each receive spiritual gifts for the edification and empowering of the church (1 Cor. 12, Acts 2). Yet women are not permitted to be elders in the church or "to teach or have authority over a man" because of Adam's priority (1 Tim. 2:11–14).

The newer view, which is sometimes called Christian feminism, agrees that men and women are of equal dignity, but it goes a step farther. Leaning heavily on a rather literal interpretation of Galatians 3:28 – "There is neither Jew nor Greek, slave nor free, male nor female, for you are all one in Christ Jesus" – it argues that gender roles have been obliterated at the cross and supplanted by the freedom that Christ brings. Proponents sometimes say that male headship was instituted at the Fall (Gen. 3:16), and that it no longer applies to a redeemed community. Christians, they say, must be free to exercise their God-given spiritual gifts without restriction; those whom God calls to lead, both male and female, must be permitted to do so for the church to fulfill its task (1 Cor. 12:7). They point to Christian women such as Priscilla (Acts 18, Rom. 16:3) as evidence that women held leadership positions in the early church. They also point to the successful ministries of women leaders and pointedly ask whether it is God's will that these be halted.

Problematic passages on the roles of women by Paul and Peter are sometimes said to speak only to specific cultural conditions at the time of writing, conditions that no longer exist. Paul's prohibition against women teaching men, for example, is said to only involve certain domineering women in the church of Ephesus. Paul's commands for women to be silent in church and cover their heads are seen as reflective of cultural practice but not binding on believers today (1 Cor. 11:1–16).

Field reports

The debate is far from academic, as many Christians have been forced to choose sides. The subject goes beyond whether Bible translations ought to have "gender-neutral" language. Indeed, the question is critical as the missions movement enters the new millennium. Questions on the roles of women in church and in the home go to the heart of what kind of churches are being planted and what kind of theology is being exported, especially in areas where feminism is not yet so pervasive.

Upholding the traditional view is the Council on Biblical Manhood and Womanhood. Advocating the newer view is the organization called Christians for Biblical Equality. What impact have such groups had on the missions enterprise?

"Little, I think," Perlman said. "Mostly I think they're preaching to their respective choirs. Significant change comes from the grass roots up. It's far more important to see what is happening on the mission field itself."[12]

The view is a bit cloudy at the moment. While opportunities for women are increasing, there is also evidence, at least in some areas, of something of a traditionalist backlash. The IFMA's Orme says increasing numbers of women are on field committees that determine mission policy in their areas of ministry, and that "a few" have been serious candidates to be field leaders. In addition, he says, a few have been named chief financial officers and personnel directors of agencies.[13]

Women are getting increasingly prominent roles in missions. Phyllis Kilbourn and Marjorie McDermid have launched a ministry, called Rainbows of Hope, to children in crisis. In February 2000, the Christian Information Network hosted the second Women's Summit on the Window, with speakers and delegates from around the world to strategize about the 10/40 Window (see chapter 7). Besa Shapllo of Albania has started a ministry offering backyard kids clubs and summer camps. Barbara Gouldsbury, an SIM missionary from New Zealand, organized a school for runaways in Khartoum.

Even complementarians sometimes agree with expanded roles for women. Janey DeMeo, a missionary who teaches at a theological institute in France and directs an orphanage in India, holds a complementarian position that says a woman may teach or even run an agency as long as she submits to a local church (and husband, if married) and is not exercising spiritual authority over men. "Women nowadays are far freer to develop diverse roles in missions and are given more liberty to explore their gifts and potential without being so stoically limited within the framework of a concept," she said. "Women are venturing into new avenues in missions."[14]

Yet even as opportunities for women are beginning to open up, other women are embracing the more traditional roles. The influence of organizations such as Focus on the Family, which extol the contributions of wives and mothers and warn of the potentially bad consequences of neglecting children, is evidently having an effect.

Cheryl Barton, a Church of God (Anderson, Ind.) missionary to Japan who holds to an egalitarian position on women's roles, has seen a shift: "There seems to be a return to an earlier era when women were expected to remain in the home to care for husband and children, and ministry was to be done by men. This 'return' is being experienced in the Southern Baptist mission in Japan. . . . And, even within our own mission, we are finding that new missionaries have this 'old' perspective on women's roles. It has completely caught me off guard, especially since I come from a group that, from its earliest days, had ministers of both sexes, ordained both, and recognized God's call to ministry upon the full body, irrespective of gender."[15]

Disputes about women's roles inevitably have an effect on the churches and agencies with which missionaries work and interact overseas. In many areas of the world outside the West, however, women face more immediate issues than whether they can lead in churches and missions agencies. They are more worried about supporting their families on meager wages, responding to physical abuse from their husbands, or being heard in society. While to some the women-in-leadership debate can appear to be a godsend, to others it seems beside the point, or even an intrusion.

Many women around the world face deadly discrimination. Unborn girls are routinely aborted in China and India – just because of their sex. Even in areas where violence against women is illegal, societies can keep culturally sanctioned homicide firmly in place. "Honor killings," dowry deaths, acid attacks, and female infanticide are among the horrors. In India, 10,000 cases of female infanticide are reported annually, while 6,000 dowry deaths were reported in 1997. The United Nations says Pakistan, India, and Bangladesh are particularly egregious offenders when it comes to tolerating violence against women. "There's violence every-where; there's gender discrimination everywhere," stated Carol Bellamy, who directs UNICEF. "But South Asia, when we assign people there, they come back raving feminists in six months."[16]

Tokunboh Adeyemo, a native of Nigeria and resident of Kenya, is general secretary of the Association of Evangelicals in Africa. He says that although women do most of the evangelism and missions work on the continent, they are "at the bottom of the pile" when it comes to training.

"We want to reverse that," Adeyemo said. "The question in Africa is not the ordination of men or the ordination of women, as the case is in the West. Women are not asking for ordination.

They are asking for recognition of their gifts from God. They want opportunities to minister and use their gifts."[17]

Barton agrees. "We must be careful not to force our culture upon other cultures," she said. "If we do, we run the risk of losing the privilege to be heard ... we must consistently share our 'light,' but allow the people with whom we're working time to accept. Sometimes they will reject. In such a case, ... I then may have to look elsewhere for a group that will accept me and my giftedness in ministry, missions, (and) leadership."[18]

The search for middle ground

At an April 1996 World Evangelical Fellowship Theological Commission consultation in London on issues facing the church in the 21st century, a mixed working group came up with a statement meant to guide the worldwide church on the subject.[19] Among its recommendations: "We recommend further theological and biblical reflection on gender issues by evangelical men and women. The lack of adequate theological resources has limited those working against abuses and exploitation of females."[20]

Is finding middle ground on such a contentious issue still possible? Corwin, a missionary with SIM, says no – not without a change of heart from both sides. "Yes, there are important biblical, hermeneutical, cultural, and historical issues that must be addressed and resolved if any kind of permanent peace is ever to exist over these matters," Corwin said. "But ... there must first be repentance and forgiveness between the sexes before we can fruitfully address the underlying issues."[21]

FURTHER READING

"Women in mission," by Gary Corwin, *EMQ*, October 1997.

"Why are there no women on the panel?" by Jim Reapsome, *World Pulse*, 5 May 1995.

Women as Risk-Takers for God, by Lorry Lutz (Grand Rapids, Baker/Carlisle: Paternoster, 1997).

"Women in Mission" theme issue, *Mission Frontiers,* August 1999.

"Recognizing God's purpose for gender distinctives in marriage and family life, church and society," *Evangelical Review of Theology,* January 1997.

Recovering Biblical Manhood and Womanhood: A Response to Evangelical Feminism, edited by John Piper and Wayne Grudem (Wheaton: Crossway Books, 1991).

DISCUSSION QUESTIONS

1. *How do you evaluate the missionary contributions of women? How have they changed over the years?*

2. *What does the Bible teach about roles and the sexes?*

3. *How might this debate impact churches overseas, positively and negatively?*

4. *How might advocates of both positions profitably work together?*

Part II

THE STRATEGIC ARENA

Chapter 7

The 10/40 Window

Frank Severn, general director of SEND International, was at a missions conference on reaching people who have had little opportunity to hear and respond to the gospel. A speaker asked a question that arrested Severn's attention: "Which is more strategic and important – to win 100 Russians to Christ, or one Uzbek?"

The speaker said the Uzbek should be the priority. How does one Uzbek outweigh 100 Russians on the missions scale? The reasoning is simple. Christianity has been present in Russia for a millennium. Even today, after 70 years of atheistic communist rule, there is a small evangelical presence firmly planted in Russian soil. The argument basically says that the Russians have had their "chance" to respond to the gospel. The Uzbeks, who are mostly Muslim, have not. God wants his name known among every people. Therefore, reaching one member of this ethnic group takes precedence over reaching 100 Russians.[1]

Such thinking is reflected in slogans like "No one deserves to hear the gospel twice until everyone has heard it once." Missions statistician David Barrett, for his part, uses a "volume of evangelism" measurement to show the imbalance of evangelistic witness around the world. For example, it is claimed that the average Russian receives 200 evangelistic invitations every year, versus one every three years for the average Uzbek. Some use these figures to justify rationing – even denying – outreach to groups that have had more than their "fair share."

Justin Long, a colleague of Barrett and the associate editor of the *World Christian Encyclopedia,* responded to Severn's qualms about ranking one Uzbek higher than 100 Russians. In a letter to *Evangelical Missions Quarterly,* Long stated, "The Uzbeks and the Russians are equally deserving of hearing the gospel. What we would like to see is more energy directed at the Uzbeks. If that means some energy must be taken away from the Russians, then so be it. With 200 opportunities a year, they have more than enough to spare."[2]

Marketing great needs

Such thinking has been encouraged and, in fact, brought to a new level in church and mission agency alike by what is known as the "10/40 Window." The 10/40 Window is an imaginary box drawn between 10 and 40 degrees of longitude, encompassing parts or all of 62 countries in Africa and Asia, and a bit of Europe. Propounded just over a decade ago by Luis and Doris Bush of the AD2000 and Beyond Movement, the Window, like any successful marketing tool, provides not only a convenient (if oversimplified) way of looking at the world, but also shows us a lot about ourselves.

Undeniably, the Window highlights areas of tremendous missiological and physical need. Some 3.1 billion people, approximately half of the world's population, live in the Window. According to Luis Bush, 55 countries there, including Uzbekistan, are classified as "least evangelized." The region is also the epicenter of the world's great non-Christian religions, including Islam, Hinduism, and Buddhism,[3] and yet it receives only 3 percent of the global missionary force and .01 percent of average Christian family income.[4]

The material needs in the Window are staggering, too. Bush offers the following statistics:

- 82 percent of the world's poorest live there;
- 23 countries there have a per-capita gross national product under $500;
- 29 countries with the lowest quality of life (based on life expectancy, infant mortality, and literacy) are there.[5]

The focus on the Window has been widespread and, on the whole, invigorating for the church. Christian leaders from more than 150 countries have prayed, strategized, and sent missionaries in response to the real needs evident in the Window.[6] While there is not space in this chapter to cover all of the initiatives related to or inspired by the Window, all the money given, and all the missionaries sent, here are a couple of examples. More information can be found at the official AD2000 and Beyond Web site, <www.ad2000.org>.

- In September 1999, about 20,000 people turned out for a world missions conference in Uberlandia, Brazil, focusing on the Window. There it was announced that 85 missionary candidates are in training for the Projecto Janela 10/40 (10/40 Window Project). The 85 come from different Latin American nations, churches, and denominations and are preparing to minister in various parts of the Window. The goal of the project is to send 1,040 Brazilian and Latin missionaries into the region by the year 2010.[7]

- Millions of Christians worldwide participated in the October 1999 "Praying through the Window IV" initiative, with the theme of "Light the Window." Previous prayer efforts for the region were held in 1993, 1995, and 1997.

Problems

Yet despite all the emphasis on the unevangelized peoples in the 10/40 Window, this powerful marketing approach has failed to make much of a missionary dent in the region's entrenched bastions of unbelief. Ralph Winter, one of the premier missions mobilizers focusing on the unreached, admitted as much during the 1997 AD2000-related Global Consultation on World Evangelization II conference in Pretoria, South Africa: "The world Christian movement has largely stalled in relation to the Hindu, Muslim, and Buddhist blocs of unreached peoples. . . . We cannot reasonably expect to achieve the marvelous goals of the AD2000 Movement without a significant change in strategy. More of the same will not be enough."[8]

The concept of the Window has developed other smudges. While a useful tool for helping Christians picture needs in a heretofore neglected area of the world, too often the Window is given a missiological, even theological, significance that it does not deserve. As we will see in chapter 9, this arbitrarily defined geographic boundary has taken on an almost mystical meaning. Luis Bush, reflecting this viewpoint, has written, "It appears evident from observation of the 10/40 Window that Satan has established a territorial stronghold with his forces to restrain the advance of the Gospel in that territory."[9]

Such thinking has certainly developed a stronghold in the minds of many people in the pews. Many churches have geared their world outreach efforts toward the Window, often to the exclusion of other, less fashionable ministries. A missions mobilizer says he heard of a church that was struggling with whether or not to back a missionary headed for Japan. The sticking point was not the character, calling, or gifts of the man. Nor was it his intended ministry. Instead, it was whether his work would be situated in the Window. Japan, it turns out, is only partly in the Window, and the church wanted to be sure the missionary's ministry was physically in the Window. Remember that the Window is a man-made creation nowhere found in the pages of Scripture. While no one disputes a church's right and responsibility to act as it believes God is directing, this is clearly an example of the tail (the Window) wagging the dog (setting priorities in missions).

Shallow thinking

Such shallow thinking in missions is more prevalent than we might like to admit. Many ministries in "traditional" mission fields are scrutinized, even dropped, if they have the misfortune of being outside the Window. Sometimes 10/40 advocates go so far as to fudge the depth of real spiritual need in some nominally

Christian countries, particularly in Europe. Some are unwilling to make a distinction between "evangelical," or those who at least theoretically hold to the Bible and have made professions of faith, and the broader sociological term "Christian." One who does, missions researcher Patrick Johnstone, author of the preeminent prayer guide *Operation World*, estimates that only 2.8 percent of Europe's 515 million people are evangelicals, including .6 percent in France, .5 percent in Austria, and .1 percent in Greece.[10] Yet the continent has had over a millennium of Christian presence, and ancient churches dot its streets, so some theorists write it off as "reached," or at least not worthy of the missions resources it currently attracts.

Reflecting this view, one researcher told an e-mail discussion group, "I would not say there are few Christians in Europe, or anywhere else. Europe on the whole is mostly Christian. France, for example, was 97 percent Christian in 1990. I think we would be more accurate to say that Christianity is widespread, but most believers do not practice their faith. This is a judgment call that is not our place to make! ... if we begin saying Europe isn't Christian, then we have greatly expanded the ... 10/40 Window frontier."

A missionary tartly replied, "If we need to expand it – even if we have to throw out the concept altogether – then so be it. Our task is to go into the whole world and make disciples."[11]

Other cautions

The 10/40 Window concept has other potential drawbacks, too. For one, it minimizes the presence and contributions of the faithful and dynamic Christians already living in the region. India, China, Egypt, and other countries there are home to millions of zealous, committed believers bringing the gospel to their neighbors and beyond. Some feel patronized or ignored by all the hubbub over the Window, particularly when it comes from the West.

For another, the militaristic or triumphalistic rhetoric from some quarters about the peoples, religions, and places of the 10/40 Window are heard and read by the people who live there. A comment about the demonic nature of Hinduism made in a 1994 issue of *Mission Frontiers* magazine was put on the Web. Before long, it ended up on a Hindu Web site and became a *cause célèbre* in India, inflaming right-wing Hindu passions against Christians.[12] In response, a number of evangelical missions leaders met in Pasadena in June 2000 for a consultation on missionary language and metaphors. During this gathering, they urged the wider missionary movement to use more care in its communications.

Third, the concept of the Window is at odds with another key missiological principle – reaching the spiritually receptive. Is it ethical to take missionaries away from regions where large numbers are entering the kingdom, such as the Philippines, in order to send them to resistant areas where the harvest is almost nonexistent? The answer should be sending more to both. Missions is not a limited pie. We need more people, more money, more resources, more thinking, and more prayer, both in the Window and around the world, until the Great Commission has been fulfilled.

Close the window?

At the launch of the third millennium, is it time to close the Window and come up with a more accurate description of a needy world? Perhaps, although like death and taxes, we will probably always have the Window with us. A better, more workable idea might be to clean the concept up a bit. All in all, the Window has helped the church focus on an area of great need. However, we need to examine our rhetoric and theology, communicate clearly to churches what the Window is and isn't, and use it judiciously in our promotions and ministries.

The need in the nations encompassed by the 10/40 Window will, and should, remain a burden for missions-minded believers.

God's glory must be shown to the billions of people in the region, whatever the cost. This will mean sending more, not fewer, missionaries and other Christians committed to evangelism there. While other regions will still need to be evangelized (or re-evangelized), the imbalance of missions personnel and resources must be addressed.

FURTHER READING

<http://www.ad2000.org>.

"Getting to the core of the core: The 10/40 Window," by Luis Bush, *Chinese in North America*, January–February 1991.

"Some thoughts on the meaning of 'all nations,'" by Frank Severn, *EMQ*, October 1997.

DISCUSSION QUESTIONS

1. *How large a role does the 10/40 Window play in your church or organization's missions strategies?*

2. *Which approach should get more priority – reaching the resistant or reaping the receptive?*

3. *Is missions a limited pie?*

4. *How could efforts be more effective in the Window?*

Chapter 8

Year 2000 Evangelism Plans

Like many jet-setting executives, Ron Cline was using his time productively while on a transatlantic flight from Frankfurt to Chicago in 1985. Cline, the head of World Radio Missionary Fellowship, was putting together a message on the power of radio to transmit the gospel around the globe. (His ministry's flagship station, HCJB in Quito, Ecuador, had been broadcasting around the world via shortwave for over half a century.) Cline noted the astounding fact that radio ministries potentially could reach 80 percent of the world's population.

Then the question came to him, "What's wrong with the *whole* world?" It was not the flight attendant. As Cline began to turn over in his mind all the standard reasons why this couldn't be done, he says he unmistakably heard the Spirit of God tell him, "Well, I want the *whole* world to know. I will *not* be satisfied with 80 percent."

For the next month back in the States those words haunted Cline. So he wrote out a commitment to provide every person on earth with an opportunity to hear the good news in a language he or she could understand. With some trepidation as the "new kid on the block" in missionary radio, Cline shared his vision with Robert Bowman, the founder of the Far East Broadcasting Company. Bowman replied, "You know, Ron, it's amazing, but God's been telling me the same thing."

The next morning Cline shared his commitment with Paul Freed, the founder and president of Trans World Radio. Freed told him, "Whoa! God has been talking to me about the same thing. We ought to do this!" Quietly, Cline asked him, "Do you think we ought to do this *together*?"

That day, 10 September, the three men signed Cline's commitment, called "World by 2000." (Other key missionary broadcasters, including SIM and Words of HOPE, have since also signed up.) Under this unprecedented agreement, they aimed to "provide every man, woman, and child on earth the opportunity to turn on their radios and hear the gospel of Jesus Christ in a language they can understand so they can become followers of Christ and responsible members of his church" by the year 2000. It was a simple, yet staggering, goal. Today, 13 organizations are involved.[1]

Deadline 2000

"World by 2000" is but one of several recent and ambitious world evangelization plans linked with the new millennium. Another, Campus Crusade's *Jesus* film, aimed to show the movie to every person in the world by the end of AD 2000. And of course there is the 800-pound gorilla of them all, the AD2000 Movement. It is a clearing house for ideas and cooperative strategies that was formally launched in 1989 at the Lausanne II international missions conference in Manila, the Philippines. AD2000's motto is "a church for every people and the gospel for every person." The movement identified 1,739 unreached people groups with at least 10,000 members, of whom less than 2 percent were evangelical believers and only 5 percent were broadly Christian (although there are exceptions on the list). In a thrust known as Joshua Project 2000, the movement set the goal of starting "at a minimum, a pioneer church planting movement within every significant ethnolinguistic people within every country of the world by 31 December 2000."[2]

"This is the first time in history that missiologists can say there is a light at the end of the tunnel," Fuller Theological Seminary's Peter Wagner said at a December 1993 conference.

"We have all the tools to fulfill the goal of the Great Commission by the end of the decade."[3]

"If we put all these [efforts] together," stated Patrick Johnstone, the author of the authoritative *Operation World* prayer guide, "it can be readily seen that the concept of availability of the gospel is far nearer being achieved than many have ever realized. Many people, of course, will not hear a Christian radio broadcast, or even see the 'Jesus' film, or maybe never learn to read so as to be touched by the written word, but the cumulative possibility of a multiplicity of ministries makes it more likely."[4]

Now that the third millennium is upon us, it is fair to ask whether we in fact have "completed" the Great Commission. And if, as it appears, we have not, then we need to find out why – not to find scapegoats, but to plan for the future.

An old dream

The dream of finishing the task has long captured the imaginations of missiologists and armchair missionaries. John R. Mott, a leading missions thinker of the late 19th and early 20th centuries, coined the watchword "The evangelization of the world in this generation." His dream was not realized, of course. The percentage of professing Christians remained basically unchanged over the course of the last century, at around 33 percent. Missionary interest declined dramatically over the next several decades after 1900, in part due to theological liberalism and World War I, but also, no doubt, because of disappointment over dashed hopes.

The fear among missions leaders today is a similar waning of missionary enthusiasm once the year 2000 euphoria wears off, as it must.

The year 2000 emphasis began, arguably, during missiologist Ralph Winter's presentation at the 1974 missions congress in Lausanne, Switzerland. The gathering, now called simply Lausanne, was called by Billy Graham to assess the state of evangelism and make plans for the future. Winter, a former engineer and the founder of the US Center for World Mission in Pasadena, California, argued that 2.7 billion of the world's people could not be won to Christ by near-neighbor evangelism. He pointed out that these people, in their various groups, had no Christian neighbors and thus could only be reached by cross-cultural missionaries.[5] Winter's emphasis on crossing cultural rather than political boundaries to spread the gospel laid the foundation for the unreached peoples movement and the AD2000 Movement, which was launched at the so-called Lausanne II congress in Manila in 1989.

Calls for caution

As the man-made deadline approached, more and more members of the international network, since renamed the AD2000 and Beyond Movement, began to de-emphasize the time element of their plans (although AD2000 has stuck to its promise to formally disband, as currently constituted, after the deadline). At the AD2000-sponsored Global Consultation on World Evangelization meetings in Seoul, South Korea, leaders placed less emphasis on the new millennium. By GCOWE II, held in 1997 in Pretoria, South Africa, many leaders were speaking of 2000 as a kind of springboard for a new century of outreach, rather than as a deadline by which to finish the task of world evangelization.

Justin Long, an associate editor of David Barrett's oft-quoted *World Christian Encyclopedia*, points out that today's Year 2000-oriented plans are nothing new in the church's history. He says that in recent years 50 new world evangelization plans have been proposed annually. Barrett and Todd Johnson estimate there have been 1,400 world evangelization plans since the time of Jesus.[6]

"I know this seems very negative," Long said, "but the fact remains that although many plans are doing an *excellent* job, they are *not* going to reach their goals. We are winning many, many battles, but if the war turned on whether the world would be evangelized, or even 'reached,' by 2000, then it would most certainly be lost."[7]

Peruvian missiologist Samuel Escobar, however, criticizes Western missions at a deeper level. In a paper read at the Iguassu Consultation on evangelical missiology held in Brazil in October 1999, Escobar wrote that some American groups have "yielded to the spirit of the age" and approach missions as "a manageable enterprise." Escobar, who teaches at Eastern Baptist Theological Seminary, calls this approach anti-theological.[8]

2000 evaluation

Here is a look at some of the other key Great Commission yardsticks and how we measure up.

Bible translation

Scripture (in the form of 960 New Testaments and 371 complete Bibles[9]) is available in 2,233 of the world's approximately 6,800 languages. At the beginning of the new millennium, 80 percent of the world's people have access to the Bible in a language they can understand. Additionally, Wycliffe Bible Translators hopes to begin work on 1,000 new languages over the next decade, and estimates that by 2025 work will have begun "in every language where Scripture is needed." Yet approximately 4,600 languages still have no portion of the Scriptures. Wycliffe estimates that if translation efforts continue at their current pace, it will take another 100 to 150 years to provide some Scripture in every language that needs it. A complicating factor, however, is that 2 billion of the people in the world cannot read the language they speak, and so literacy efforts must be added to many translation projects.

Christian radio

The World By 2000 radio initiative was launched in 1985 to provide Christian programming to the 279 megalanguages with at least a million speakers who had no access to such programming. Currently, only 91 of these languages still lack a gospel witness by radio, and this number is being reduced by an estimated 10 to 15 languages each year. However, World By 2000 has changed its name to World By Radio, in recognition of the fact that the original goal has not been met. Indeed, more languages are being added to the list every year as populations swell.[10]

James F. Engel, who is perhaps more responsible than anyone for introducing marketing concepts to the missions enterprise, says we need to be cautious when it comes to claiming vast evangelistic successes with media tools. "In the case of electronic media, it would be unusual for 15 to 20 percent of a given audience even to have their radios or TVs on, let alone for them to pay attention, comprehend, and respond," Engel wrote in an article in *Christianity Today*. "This fact has been documented in thousands of studies. . . . We have discovered over the years that people are equally selective in responding to Christian programming, especially when receptivity is low. Obviously, the Holy Spirit can and does override this human tendency, but it is presumptuous to contend that technology will suddenly enable us to bypass normal limitations."[11]

The Jesus film

The film has been seen by 2.6 billion people in 547 languages, an increase of 404 languages in a decade. However, it is no panacea. "These tools are wonderful when they are used as bridges to presenting the gospel and seeds for planting the gospel, but when they are seen as ends in themselves, they diminish severely the crucial human element in evangelism and discipleship," notes Paul Borthwick of Development Associates International.[12]

Church planting

Dawn Ministries derives its name from the concept of "Discipling A Whole Nation." Dawn's approach is to encourage saturation church planting, in which Christian leaders in a country agree to cooperate to start congregations until every small community has an evangelizing church. Three major evangelical groups – the World Evangelical Fellowship, the Lausanne Committee for World Evangelization, and AD2000 – have endorsed the DAWN concept.

Dawn-oriented initiatives exist or are taking shape in 150 countries, 60 of which have set a total goal of starting 3 million churches. In those 60, a million churches have been planted in the last 10 years. Jim Montgomery, founder of Dawn Ministries, hoped to see 7 million churches started through the movement by the end of the 20th century. Yet even if somehow that goal were achieved, these congregations would not be capable of finishing the task. Yet Montgomery, who in 1985 gave up a secure ministry to found his organization, believes the Great Commission is doable.

"We don't know, and the Lord didn't make it plain, exactly what the Great Commission would look like when it was completed," Montgomery said. "But, yes, I believe it was a specific command. Therefore, he wants us to do it."[13]

Assessment

In an article for *Evangelical Missions Quarterly*, Robertson McQuilkin, chancellor of Columbia International University and a former missionary to Japan, asked the question, "Are we winning or losing?" On the one hand, McQuilkin said, are the optimists who believe the church is close to fulfilling the Great Commission. They point out that when William Carey, the father of modern missions, set sail for India two centuries ago, the ratio of unsaved people to Bible-believing Christians was 49 to one. This decade it is a much more encouraging nine to one, with the vast majority of that growth occurring in the non-Western world.

On the other hand, McQuilkin pointed to the pessimists who see the multitudes of people beyond the reach of the gospel.

"Angle the statistics in an optimistic way and speak theoretically in percentages, and we are winning the war," McQuilkin said. "Look at the task remaining in terms of the sheer numbers of people who will live somewhere forever, and who now have no chance to hear, and the cause seems hopeless.

"Both truths are needed: The task remaining is vastly greater than it ever was before. But the resources and momentum to do it are greater, too."[14]

Over the last several years the leaders and strategists behind the most promising plans have begun squelching the idea (that they started) that their efforts can bring "closure" to the Great Commission by the self-imposed deadline of 2000. As has happened too often in the past when evangelism goals have not been met, some leaders seem all too willing to say of their particular plan, "Well, it was only a *goal*." They point to the people mobilized and brought into God's kingdom and don't seem too eager to have their results scrutinized. Sometimes, they just move on to the next plan.

Jay Gary points out that "it appears that since GCOWE '95 some have modulated their tone. Instead of promising a full-blown church-planting movement among every remaining unreached people by 2000, they now seem to be talking about 'minimal' goals for 2000. Rather than 'A Church for Every People' people are describing these goals as 'A Prayer for Every People,' or 'A Team for Every People' by the year 2000."[15]

The danger is that with the goal having been so clearly set for the year 2000, it will be very evident that it has not been met. Not every person has heard the gospel; not every people group has a church. Some in missions warn of a massive letdown when the task remains unfinished beyond the deadline.

David Hesselgrave, considered by some to be the dean of American evangelical missiologists, thanks God for the significant role various campaigns, strategies, and tools have played in accomplishing Christian mission. But that is not the end of the story. He says the various plans of post-World War II missions need to be carefully and objectively analyzed.

"It's impossible to calculate the benefits that could accrue to our successors were they to know the strengths and weaknesses of these proposals, and where they succeeded and where they failed," Hesselgrave said. "A leading African theologian-missiologist maintains that American strategists will never allow for such studies. Time may prove him to be correct. But older missiologists will remember when [church growth expert] George Peters was allowed, and even encouraged, to do an extensive critique of saturation evangelism [techniques] and Evangelism-in-Depth in particular." (EID is a citywide approach that was developed and has been used extensively in Latin America.)

"It proved to be a most helpful study," Hesselgrave continued. "Let us hope that, with hundreds of masters and doctoral students searching for viable research projects, there will be many more such studies. Why should 21st-century mission leaders spend inordinate amounts of time and money inventing and reinventing the wheel?"[16]

Perhaps these latest global evangelization plans should be compared to the prolonged air attacks that pounded Saddam Hussein's military during the Gulf War: necessary, but not sufficient. The ground troops still had to go in and put their lives on the line in Iraq. The same holds true on the missions front. Radio, the *Jesus* film, prayer, Bible translation, and strategizing about the unreached are all good and needed tasks. However, they are no substitute for the man or woman willing to fight the daily spiritual battle in the trenches, risking life, limb, and honor to glorify God's name among the nations.

Ron Cline acknowledges that even as the World By Radio broadcasters have made and continue to make impressive strides, the horizon continues to recede before them, as one language after another crosses the million-person threshold. But he isn't depressed or frustrated. "We can't orchestrate when the Lord's going to return anyway," Cline said. "We're doing our best and hope he'll find us faithful when he comes. What we're trying to do is get the gospel to everybody.... There's no room for discouragement these days. God is on the march. He's doing amazing things. More people will hear the gospel of Christ today than at any time in the history of the world."[17]

FURTHER READING

"Mission possible," by Stan Guthrie, *New Man*, June 1997.

"A church for every people – beyond 2000," by Jay Gary, *EMQ*, July 1996.

AD2025 Global Monitor, edited by David Barrett and Todd M. Johnson.

"State of the World 2000," *Mission Frontiers*, June 2000.

"Welcome to A.D. 2000: Now what?" by Stan Guthrie, *World Pulse*, 7 January 2000.

DISCUSSION QUESTIONS

1. *What role does a calendar deadline play in your church or agency's world evangelization plans?*

2. *How successful do you believe the various Year 2000 plans have been?*

3. *What effect do you think the church's failure to fulfill the Great Commission will have on missionary motivation? What effect should it have?*

4. *What should the church do differently in the 21st century than it did in the 20th in regard to missions?*

Chapter 9

Prayer as Warfare

Kenyan pastor Thomas Muthee and his wife, Margaret, saw the notorious Nairobi suburb of Kiambu as a ministry graveyard. Searching for solutions to Kiambu's violence and the barriers to Christian outreach, in 1988 the Muthees began praying and doing research on the cause of the spiritual oppression. Finally, Thomas Muthee says, they discovered the source of Kiambu's oppression – the spirit of witchcraft. The locus was said to be a diviner named Mama Jane.

Muthee held an evangelistic crusade, and 200 people made public Christian commitments. Soon the church they formed, called the Prayer Cave, sponsored 24-hour prayer for Kiambu from its grocery store basement location. Mama Jane fought back but eventually left town, defeated. Muthee says that "the demonic influence – the principality over Kiambu – was broken." Since then, the church has grown to 5,000 members, 400 of whom meet daily for 6 a.m. prayer sessions. The crime rate in Kiambu is down and the economy and population are growing.[1]

In another case, the results of a focus on the demonic were not so positive. Patrick Johnstone, the respected author of *Operation World*, is a missionary with WEC International. He gives the following account of what happened: "One of our most effective church planting missionaries had become so involved with delivering Christians from demons. . . . She claimed that thousands of demons had to be cast out of pastors in her many months of ministry around the country. This ministry was causing dismay to many, and appeared to be even possibly a sidetracking of the enemy into endless conversations with demons and time-consuming deliverances. She was even cross-examining lesser demons to find out more concerning the upper echelons of the demonic hierarchy. We sought to warn her of the real dangers associated with the latter and the need for a rounded balance in ministry in the former. I cannot help but feel that she was laying herself open to believing the lies and distortions of the enemy and having all her energies consumed in this deliverance ministry. She took some of our advice and moderated some of the excesses in her ministry."[2]

With good reason did C. S. Lewis pen his famous dictum: "There are two equal and opposite errors into which our race can fall about the devils. One is to disbelieve in their existence. The other is to believe, and to feel an excessive and unhealthy interest in them."[3]

Excessive and unhealthy interest?

In Lewis's day, of course, the prevailing error, born of the conceit of modernism, was to disbelieve in demons. Today, in our postmodern era, the risk, even for Christians, is to develop an unhealthy interest in them. The occult is all around us, packaged seductively in movies and television programs like *Buffy the Vampire Slayer*, *Angel*, and *The Blair Witch Project*, and in books like Napoleon Hill's *Think and Grow Rich*. The church in general, and the missions movement in particular, have not been immune.

In recent decades missions theorists like C. Peter Wagner and Charles Kraft have embraced a more supernaturalistic paradigm concerning the activity of Satan and his minions – and how Christians can fight it. Prayer used to be directed to God; today, as often as not, it seems to be directed against demons.

This paradigm, known broadly as the spiritual warfare movement, seemingly has been validated by the spectacular results reported by evangelists like Ed Silvoso and Carlos Annacondia of Argentina. Yet many in the evangelical missions movement are asking hard questions.

While in earlier missions eras prayer was seen primarily as a way to communicate one's needs to God, as a way to join God in his saving purposes for the world, and as a proving ground for one's faith, today prayer is often viewed as a tool to "bind" demonic "strongholds" holding people, cities, and nations in spiritual bondage. This strategy is supplemented by "spiritual mapping," the discipline of uncovering the spiritual infrastructure of a city or region, which determines its spiritual direction.

The spiritual warfare mentality has had a profound effect on missions. Massive events such as Praying Through the Window I (1993), II (1995), III (1997), and IV (1999), prayer journeys to the 100 Gateway Cities of the 10/40 Window (see chapter 7), the launch of organizations like Global Harvest Ministries, and cooperative ventures such as the International Spiritual Warfare Network have involved and immersed millions in this worldview. The United Prayer Track of the AD2000 and Beyond Movement was dominated by this outlook. Some $6.5 million was spent to construct a state-of-the-art World Prayer Center in Colorado Springs in 1998.

Wagner, a professor at Fuller Theological Seminary's School of World Mission and an expert in church growth principles, has been called "the apostle of the world prayer movement over this last decade."[4] Wagner has also been accused of promoting a sub-biblical, even animistic, worldview. Wagner's certainty about unseen spiritual realities can be disconcerting for Christians used to finding their doctrines solely in the Bible. Wagner and others in this camp claim the Bible as their starting point, of course. They construct their theology around verses such as Daniel 10:13, 2 Corinthians 4:4, Ephesians 6:12, and the descriptions of Jesus' encounters with the demonic. They say they are studying spiritual dynamics largely hidden from the church in its 2,000 years of existence.

A key element in their understanding is the idea of territorial spirits, or fallen angels that hold sway over cities, regions, and countries and control people's spiritual receptiveness to the gospel. Their approach is to identify such "strongholds" and come against them in the name of Christ. Once these demons are removed or neutralized, the theory goes, people will be more open to spiritual truth.

Wagner led a group of intercessors in prayer for the ancient city of Ephesus for a year before holding a Celebration Ephesus worship service for 5,000 people from 62 countries on site in October 1999, complete with a 100-voice choir, 16-piece orchestra, shofars, "Levitical trumpeters," banners, and dancers.[5] While praise was a major element of Celebration Ephesus, in the months leading up to the event Wagner said his covert goal for the event was to come against an entity he calls the Queen of Heaven, worshipped in Abraham's hometown of Ur of the Chaldees. This "queen," according to Wagner and associates, has also been known as the pagan goddess Diana, worshipped in Ephesus in New Testament times.

"Recent spiritual mapping has revealed that one of the Queen of Heaven's major strongholds, if not the principal one, is located in ancient Ephesus, Turkey," Wagner stated in an e-mail prior to Celebration Ephesus. "I have come to the conclusion that the spiritual principality under Satan most responsible through history for keeping men and women in spiritual darkness, blinding their minds to the gospel of Christ, has been the Queen of Heaven, mentioned in Jeremiah 7:16–18. . . . The Queen of Heaven has set up strongholds and power points in virtually every nation of the world in order to keep the maximum number of individuals in spiritual darkness."[6]

Following Celebration Ephesus, an associate of Wagner, Chuck Pierce, stated, "You could actually hear by the Spirit of the Lord an unlocking in the nations of the earth for his planned, future Harvest."[7]

Despite the fact that the 10/40 Window remains one of the poorest and least evangelized regions on earth, Wagner now says that God has told him it is time to move on to a new one, the so-called 40/70 Window, which covers Turkey, Europe, and Central Asia. A more balanced focus on this area is certainly welcome, but Wagner plans to direct much of his effort there to combating the Queen of Heaven.[8]

Tough questioning

It is no wonder that this experience-oriented approach has come under harsh criticism from other evangelicals. "To accept the validity of an experience and to draw inferences from it, is often to accept unwittingly animistic and magical beliefs implicit in the experience itself," write Robert Priest, Thomas Campbell, and Bradford Mullen in a hard-hitting critique: "Many missionaries and missiologists unwittingly have internalized and are propagating animistic and magical notions of spirit power which are at odds with biblical teaching, using such notions as the basis for missiological method."[9] Meanwhile, the Intercession Working Group of the Lausanne Committee for World Evangelization says the spiritual warfare emphasis carries the risk of leading us "to think and operate on pagan world views."[10]

Calling Christian brothers and sisters animistic is a serious charge, but what exactly is animism? Animism is amoral and power-conscious to the core. Animists seek to control their destinies by controlling or appeasing, through sacrifice and ritual, the spirit beings that they believe animate the cosmos. For purposes of this discussion, here is a definition: "Animism is a method for the integration of man with himself and nature. To achieve this situation the devotee seeks a source of power. The animist acknowledges an ideal state, and that he is estranged from that state, and that beliefs and practices will lead to a return to wholeness."[11]

Philip Steyne, a professor of missions at Columbia International University, says that, as practiced, every religion has elements of animism, not just tribal systems assigning spiritual powers to observable phenomena.

Proponents of the spiritual warfare approach, such as Kraft,[12] respond on a number of levels. First, they accuse their critics of being captive, or nearly so, to a Western, Enlightenment era paradigm that automatically excludes the supernatural. Essentially, they say, critics see the movement through naturalistic lenses. Second, they say that the spiritual warfare approach to missions *works*. They point to deliverances and lives transformed following such encounters, and sometimes claim that the critics have no such data to appeal to. Third, they say that the approach is needed because of the manifest failure of Western missions, both in spreading the gospel widely and in using it to transform people's lives and worldviews. Kraft points to the many so-called "Christians" around the world who have committed themselves to Christ and yet "continue to go to shamans, diviners and the like to meet their felt need for spiritual power.... The gospel message has encountered them at the point of allegiance and they study the Scriptures to discover God's truths but they have not come to experience anything within Christianity that confronts and replaces their previous sources of spiritual power."[13] Fourth, to the charge that the approach is not explicitly taught in the Bible and therefore is not biblical, they contend that if it is not explicitly condemned in the Bible, then it might be biblical. The fact that modern science, for example, is not found within the pages of Scripture does not invalidate it. They claim that just as scientists study the principles of the physical universe, they are uncovering the principles of the spiritual universe.

Needless to say, not everyone agrees. Charles R. A. Hoole of Colombo Theological Seminary cites a practical problem with the movement – many of the so-called territorial spirits are of human origin. He cites the example of the village god Bandara Deiyo in Kandy, Sri Lanka (modeled after the district governor position), and Prabhupada, worshipped as a deity in Durban, South Africa, but actually the deceased founder of the Hare Krishnas.

"The idea of 'territorial spirits' is pagan," Hoole said. "It depicts a world peopled by gods, a world full of chaos and terror, but made safe by the manipulative powers of shamans."[14]

Problems and solutions

Much of the momentum for spiritual warfare comes from Frank Peretti's novels *This Present Darkness* and *Piercing the Darkness*. Wagner admits, "Undoubtedly, the single most influential event that has stimulated interest in strategic-level spiritual warfare was the publication of Frank Peretti's two novels."[15] These depict a God who lets angels and demons "duke it out" while remaining largely on the sidelines. Much of the spiritual warfare movement implies the existence of a God who is either unwilling or unable to work without specific, targeted prayers to first neutralize the satanic hosts pervading the planet.

If this is in any way representative of our thinking, what kind of a God are we presenting to the world? Is he the awesome, sovereign Lord of Scripture? If not, why should good Muslims, animists, Hindus, atheists, and Buddhists abandon their own gods, flee their sins, and cling to Christ? If, as some say, God is dependent on us to accomplish his work, how can we hope that his mission in the world will indeed be victorious?

We need to recover our understanding of God as the sovereign King of kings and Lord of lords, as Scripture consistently depicts him to be, and as the Protestant Reformation rediscovered him to be. Timothy George has suggested that William Carey's missionary vision sprang from his bedrock Calvinist convictions,[16] setting the stage for the incredible growth of today's worldwide missionary movement. Going even further, author and pastor John Piper says biblical hope, based on God's sovereignty, "gripped the Puritan mind and eventually gave birth to the modern missionary movement in 1793. William Carey was nourished on this tradition, as were David Brainerd and Adoniram Judson, Alexander Duff and David Livingstone, John Paton and a host of others who gave their lives to reach the unreached peoples of the world. The modern missionary movement did not arise in a theological vacuum. It grew out of a great reformation tradition that put the sovereignty of God square in the center of human life."[17]

Neglecting the awesome truth of God's sovereignty in missions has made our efforts possibly less effective, and certainly less God-honoring, than they might have been. John Orme had it right when he called for "a restoring of our Reformation distinctives. The command of Christ must be accompanied by commitment to *sola scriptura*, *sola gratia*, and *sola fide*, in the totality of our organizational ethos. This will be our only defense against current excesses and shallow thoughts about relationships."[18] And as George Whitefield told John Wesley, we all should seek the truth that "shall most debase man and exalt the Lord Jesus. Nothing but the doctrines of the Reformation can do this."[19]

But won't an emphasis on the Reformation alienate many evangelicals of more Arminian conviction? As John Piper has wisely pointed out: "As much as we would like it, we do not have the luxury of living in a world where the most nourishing truths are unopposed. If we think that we can suspend judgment on all that is controversial and feed our souls on only what is left, we are living in a dream world. There is nothing left."[20]

Another Reformation doctrine that might need to be dusted off is total depravity. Adherence to this doctrine will protect us from some of the woollier notions of the spiritual warfare movement, such as this contention by George Otis of the Sentinel Group: "Because all human peoples belong to God initially by right of fatherhood, Satan has no automatic control over them. Unless individuals give themselves over to the rulership of Satan willingly, they will remain under the tender influence of the Holy Spirit."[21] Not only does this idea contradict the notion of original sin, it flies in the face of verses which claim that Satan is the spiritual father of unbelievers (John 8:44), whose minds he has blinded to the light of Christ (2 Cor. 4:4–6). Quick-fix spiritual warfare-type solutions to the sinful resistance of peoples are unlikely to gain much traction in darkened human hearts.

"Warfare" and Scripture

A major problem is the spiritual warfare movement's loose connection with Scripture. Claiming the truthfulness of a teaching based on recent experience or a new revelation is the *modus operandi* of a cult, not of biblical Christianity. False religions always have something normative in addition to the Bible. As Mike Wakely, Operation Mobilization area director for South

Asia, has said, "Once the basic criterion of scriptural truth has been replaced by the extra-biblical basis of personal experience, imagination, and feeling, the sky is the limit as to where this teaching could take excitable people."[22]

The Apostle Paul said, "All Scripture is God-breathed and is useful for teaching, rebuking, correcting and training in righteousness, so that the man of God may be thoroughly equipped for every good work" (2 Tim. 3:16–17). Since this is so, where does this new doctrine come from? If this "warfare" emphasis was not known or needed in the church's first two millennia, why would it be for the third millennium? And if it is a true way of becoming "equipped for every good work," why did God take so long to reveal it? And how do proponents defend themselves against the charge that they are promoting just the latest gnostic teaching in the church? Gnosticism, long a bane of the church, is an approach to faith that says that some special, hidden knowledge available only to the few is necessary to properly live the Christian life or to do God's will. The warfare emphasis certainly seems to imply this.

Conclusion

Despite its flaws, it would be a mistake to dismiss the spiritual warfare movement out of hand. For one thing, the Western church (including the missions enterprise) needs to be reminded over and over that "our struggle is not against flesh and blood, but against the rulers, against the authorities, against the powers of this dark world and against the spiritual forces of evil in the heavenly realms" (Eph. 6:12). Confronting the satanic influences so evident in the Nazi Germanys, Kosovos, and Rwandas of this world without the power and authority given to us by Christ is futile at best, dangerous at worst. The spiritual warfare movement rightly reminds us that we battle not only the world and the flesh, but the devil as well.

The warfare movement has also brought untold millions into the larger missions movement, "praying through the Window," "marching for Jesus," and going on "prayer walks." God has certainly used those sincere prayers as they have been directed to him. There are signs of spiritual openness in places formerly closed to the gospel, from the Arab Muslim world to the former Soviet Union, and who is to say how much of the credit does or does not accrue to Wagner and company? As James 5:16b says, "The prayer of a righteous man is powerful and effective." Prayer remains a critical element in world evangelization. Perhaps some of the theology is a bit off; yet God can and does honor imperfect prayers.

And while some of the activity has, no doubt, been un-productive from a ministry perspective, it still may lead to significant ministry. Someone spending lots of time and money on a trip to pray against the spirits said to be controlling an unevangelized area may come home with an idea for reaching orphans there or feeding the homeless or starting a church.

I went through a similar process, not with respect to spiritual warfare but with popular "end times" literature. When I was a new Christian, I scoured the papers for signs of the "revived Roman Empire" (the European Common Market) and the Antichrist (Kissinger, Sadat?). There was little separating my faith from an apocalyptic reading of the headlines. Though this introduction to Christianity was great fun, it provided a flimsy foundation for discipleship. It also encouraged apathy about the world God created. Yet today I am involved in ministries to help people's bodies and souls, while a little less certain about end-times chronologies.

Perhaps many in the spiritual warfare movement will make a similar pilgrimage. That would be preferable to a continued excessive and unhealthy interest in the demonic.

FURTHER READING

"A critical look at a new 'key' to evangelization," by Mike Wakely, *EMQ*, April 1995.

Territorial Spirits and World Evangelisation?, by Chuck Lowe (Sevenoaks, Kent: OMF International, 1998).

God at War: The Bible and Spiritual Conflict, by Gregory A. Boyd (Downers Grove: InterVarsity Press, 1999).

Spiritual Power and Missions: Raising the Issues, edited by Edward Rommen (Pasadena: William Carey Library, 1995).

Touch the World Through Prayer, by Wesley Duewel (Grand Rapids: Zondervan, 1986).

DISCUSSION QUESTIONS

1. *Define the characteristics of the spiritual warfare movement.*
2. *What are the movement's strengths and weaknesses?*
3. *How should missionaries respond to this movement?*
4. *What will be the movement's effect on Christians and churches overseas?*

Chapter 10

The Short-Term Missions Explosion

A veteran Christian teacher in Beijing has had enough of short-term visitors from her home country. "I used to think I could give them a briefing and orientation that could be helpful," she told a mission agency leader. "Very few ever listened. They all have their own agenda. All they want is instant results." The woman now refuses to meet with such people and does not consider them to really be ministering to China.[1]

In Kenya, a work team brought a missionary couple nearly to tears, reports Andrew Atkins of Emmanuel International. "They lived way out in the bush and one of their few luxuries was a carefully rationed stock of peanut butter," he said. "It wasn't just that the team quickly consumed all the peanut butter, but how they did it – hogging it down and asking for more, then complaining when they ran out."

Another time, Atkins says, a team went to Nairobi to work with slum dwellers. When the members returned home they talked about "how we were able to love the people." What they may not have mentioned was their choice to wear rubber surgical gloves while doing ministry in order to avoid the diseases of those among whom they worked.[2]

Such tensions are increasingly common, not only between short-term workers and their career missionary brethren, but also between short-termers and so-called "national" believers. Jim Raymo of WEC International expresses the skepticism of many in the traditional sending agencies when he says, "short-term efforts without language and culture learning will not yield long-term results."[3]

A new option

Short-term ministry is an option few other generations of Western Christians, much less their non-Western counterparts, ever considered. William Carey spent more than three decades in northern India without so much as a furlough (what we now often call a "home ministry assignment"). Nineteenth-century missionaries to West Africa packed their belongings in wooden coffins, never expecting to return to their homelands. They were short-term workers only in the sense that many of them died within a few years, some within months, of their arrival in that malaria-ridden region.

Diving into the deep end of world missions without putting at least a toe in the water is unthinkable to most boomers, however. Gone are the days when a missionary speaker would make an appeal from a pulpit and his hearers would jump up and volunteer for "the field." Unanswered questions and potential problems – Will I be able to raise my support? Will I get culture shock? Will I be able to use my gifts? – used to be dealt with during long-term ministry. Now they are dealt with before the ministry starts – or, if possible, during a short-term trip.

Part of the reason for this change is a generational difference between earlier builders of missions and today's young and middle-aged adults. As has been well documented elsewhere, baby boomers and busters are less likely to support an enterprise, either financially or personally, without firsthand knowledge of it. Many are interested in projects – the more tangible the better. And that most emphatically includes missions. Putting up a new school or showing the *Jesus* film to some refugees sounds a lot more doable to them than painstakingly learning the language, religion, and culture of a people.

So we now find organizations such as the Finishers Project, which aims to plug mid-career and retired professionals into missions. Meanwhile "teen teams" and college students work on targeted projects, teams of skilled builders construct churches and camps overseas, short-termers teach in missionary kid schools and help in leadership training. Jim Reapsome, editor-at-large for *Evangelical Missions Quarterly* and *World Pulse*, says, "Churches have developed significant avenues of service with adult teams working from two weeks to two months. Among career missionaries, more of them are working as teams on specific projects, collaborating with church leaders on the field."[4]

Trends

Short-term work had its genesis about four decades ago with the launch of two organizations employing short-termers: Operation Mobilization and Youth With A Mission. The explosion in short-term workers from the West has been remarkable in the last two decades. The Mission Advanced Research and Communi-cation Center (MARC) of World Vision has estimated that the number of US lay people involved in short-term projects increased from 22,000 in 1979 to 120,000 in 1989.[5] Later estimates held that 250,000 were sent out in 1992, and 450,000 in 1998.[6] The *Mission Handbook*, meanwhile, says the number of short-termers sent by mission agencies and serving from two weeks to a year increased from 38,968 in 1992 to 63,995 in 1996[7] to 100,386 in 1999.[8] It also notes that of the roughly 40,000 cross-cultural missionaries sent by US Protestant agencies, roughly 7,000 are short-termers serving one to four years.[9] These figures, of course, do not take into account the long-term missionaries who leave the field during or at the end of their first term of service (the standard is four years).

One explanation for the surge in short-term missionaries is that the definition of "missionary" is being stretched in what one might call the democratization of missions. (Ralph Winter of the US Center for World Mission, however, calls it the amateurization of missions.) Seth Barnes, executive director of the short-term agency Adventures in Missions, writes, "These changes are forcing a redefinition of our concept of a missionary. No longer is the mission field viewed as the province of an elite few. Increasingly, ordinary lay people are finding that they can be empowered to contribute to the missions enterprise with their time and talent."[10]

James Engel, one of the most astute watchers of missions trends in the North American church, asserts in his 1989 book *Baby Boomers and the Future of World Missions*, "A short-term missionary service program is a must. Organizations not providing this option will face a manpower crisis."[11]

Concerns

Proponents of short-term missionary service often assert that these missionaries will later enlarge the pool of long-term, career missionaries. Engel claims that "prior short-term service on the field sharply increases interest in a missionary career."[12]

Yet while the number of short-termers has increased, the number of career workers has leveled off or declined. Even financial giving to agencies, which one might reasonably expect to grow with the bulging ranks of those who have gone on overseas ministry projects, has remained static, at less than $3 billion in inflation-adjusted dollars annually.[13]

Yet that is not the whole financial story. STEM Ministries, a short-term sending agency, has surveyed former participants and found that their prayer and giving increased significantly after their participation on a trip.[14] Leslie Pelt, a missionary to Nigeria, has concerns about the justification for short-term missions on the basis of generational differences. She comments tartly, "We seem to be saying that because baby boomers are different, missions should be different. However, the cost of discipleship has not changed."[15]

"Short-term missionaries do not really get to know us," an African believer told missionary Jim Lo. "We may love them as brothers and sisters, but they are still strangers to us. It is hard to be influenced by strangers. We need more long-term missionaries than short-term missionaries."

Ajith Fernando, national director of Youth for Christ in Sri Lanka, comments that many of today's missionaries seem to have an aversion to struggle. "Unfortunately, they don't try to radically identify with the people," he said. "Coming only for short terms, they live as foreigners in Sri Lanka – quite removed from the people and ignorant of their struggles. Often those who join them hope that some of the missionary riches will trickle down. . . . They are taken for a ride by the people who joined with them in the hope of exploiting their wealth. . . . One of the biggest problems in missions today is the 'softness' of the missionaries going out from affluent countries."[16]

Another concern about the work of short-term missionaries is expressed by David Mays, Midwest regional director of Advancing Churches in Missions Commitment, who fears that "issues of preparation and follow-up are woefully neglected."[17]

Still others fear that short-term workers are draining the money and talents that would otherwise go to long-term work. But Tom Steller, missions pastor of Bethlehem Baptist Church in Minneapolis, doesn't subscribe to the limited-pie theory of short-term missions. He is all for the boom. "This is thrilling to me," he said. "I think it is a stimulation to missions. I don't think it is robbing missions dollars from long-term missionaries but rather widening the pool of informed missions supporters, both the returning short-termers as well as the support networks they have tapped into."[18]

Effective and pleasing

Short-term work, whether two weeks or two years, can indeed be effective and pleasing to God. Yes, it can cost a lot of money, disrupt nationals and missionaries, encourage short-term thinking, and inoculate some against career missions involvement. But done well, it can open participants' eyes to the sometimes gritty realities of the world, make them aware of their own ethno-centrism and the gifts and courage of non-Western believers, and spark a lifelong commitment to missions. In the best cases, some real kingdom work gets done, too.

An example of how this can be done is provided by College Church in Wheaton.[19] The church aims to have half of its adult members participate in short-term missions trips. The church's goal is to match its operating domestic budget and its missions budget. The church has an extensive short-term program, called STAMP (Short-Term Adult Mission Program). Not just any short-term approach will do, however. Almost every team, in consultation with a missionary supported by the church, does a ministry or project that will directly support the work of a College Church missionary. One team may lead a vacation Bible school for missionary kids. Another may do evangelism in the UK, while another builds a school. All attempt to do things that free missionaries to do their jobs more effectively.

Jim Lo, a former missionary to Southern Africa and Cambodia and currently a missions professor at Indiana Wesleyan University, lists a number of blessings that accompany short-termers: encouragement to missionaries and national churches, vision for missions, and partnership ministries with missionaries. He says simply, "Short-term missionaries are needed."[20]

Effect on goers

Paul Borthwick, a senior associate with Development Associates International, strongly supports such ministry for the good it will do participants. He says a short-term trip will expand your view of God, cause you to see what you own differently, give you a clearer idea of hardship, give you a fresh look at heaven, stretch your faith, and force you to grow.[21]

In my own case, a 12-day evangelism trip to Poland gave me valuable experience sharing my faith in a cross-cultural setting, introduced me to the stresses and joys of support raising on a small scale, gave me a small taste of culture shock, and opened my mind to a small part of God's world. In fact, my wife and I still maintain contact with our translator.

Unfortunately, our team was not perfect. Some members seemed more interested in throwing water balloons from the windows of the youth hostel we stayed in or shopping for bargains than in learning to understand a people shaped by centuries of oppression. Did we turn Poland upside down for Jesus? Hardly, but we were changed and strengthened as we saw God work and provide. Would all these benefits and more have occurred without the trip? I doubt it. And, best of all, my wife Christine and I hope one day to be reunited in heaven with one of the people we shared the gospel with in a Krakow park one day.

Suggestions

Some missionaries recommend that trips be at least six months to a year. One says 18 months is best, because that length allows one to experience (and get over) culture shock. Only then can you realistically discover whether you have the gifts and calling to be a long-term missionary. Another says that prospects must seek a good fit between their skills, gifts, and sense of calling and a short-term assignment. Writing in the *Askamissionary* e-mail newsletter, Jim Hogrefe of OMS International says, "Determine whether or not the short-term trip will stimulate career missionary work or if it is mostly just a one-time project."[22]

Short-term missions, however, is not a one-time phenomenon. The missions landscape has changed, and mission agencies that adapt to it, while remaining faithful to biblical principles, will prosper.

As Atkins notes, "Work teams are here to stay. Research tells us that, churches tell us that, experience tells us that. So let's make the necessary sacrifices to make them better. Out of these teams will probably come the leaders of our missions in the next century."[23]

FURTHER READING

"Work teams? No, 'taste and see' teams," by Andrew Atkins, *EMQ*, October 1991.

"What's behind the wave of short-termers?" by Leslie Pelt, *EMQ*, October 1992.

"The changing face of the missionary force," by Seth Barnes, *EMQ*, October 1992.

"The editorial of Ralph D. Winter," *Mission Frontiers*, March–April 1996.

"Short-term missions boom," by John Maust, *Latin America Evangelist*, April–June 1991.

Mission Handbook, 1998–2000, edited by John Siewert and Edna Valdez (Monrovia: MARC, 1998).

"Some thoughts on missionary burnout," by Ajith Fernando, *EMQ*, October 1999.

"Short-term missions: is it worth it?" by Susan G. Loobie, *Latin America Evangelist*, January–March 2000.

"The short-term missions movement," *Mission Frontiers* theme issue, January 2000.

DISCUSSION QUESTIONS

1. *Is your church or agency focused primarily on short-term or long-term ministry?*
2. *What are some of the strengths and weaknesses of short-term missions?*
3. *How can you make your short-term ministries more effective?*
4. *Do you find the reasons given in support of short-term missions to be valid biblically?*

Chapter 11

Partnerships

Not long ago at a city park in a Central American nation, missionary Patrick McDonald spotted a group of 30 street children. He was heartened to see a group of Christians begin ministering to the kids. Then, as he watched, another group of Christians arrived, then another, all within half an hour. All were targeting the same group of 30 kids.

Another time McDonald discovered that five soup kitchens in one city in South America were providing food to poor children. However, all five ministries offered food only on Mondays. None was available the rest of the week.

There are an estimated 1.8 billion "at risk" children around the world. The evangelical presence trying to help them, though inadequate to meet every need, is considerable. McDonald estimates there are 110,000 full-time workers and 20,000 ministries to children worldwide, though not all are for children in crisis – the homeless, refugees, exploited. Some 2 million "at risk" youngsters are being cared for every day under the auspices of evangelical ministries. Yet until recently there has been little cooperation among these ministries. McDonald says that, for the sake of the children, and our integrity as Christians, it is time to change.

McDonald has been instrumental in founding the Viva Network, an Oxford-based international partnership movement. It has been endorsed by the World Evangelical Fellowship (WEF), the Lausanne Committee for World Evangelization, and the AD2000 and Beyond Movement. Viva has helped to set up dozens of national networks, has held a series of conferences, and has produced ministry resources that have been widely accepted. WEF has been influenced to launch a children's commission to focus ministry efforts on the problem, as has the Association of Evangelicals in Africa.

"People are starting to look at the Christian community of outreach to children as that – a community," McDonald stated. "There is a strong sense of coming together, of a need to network and share resources, ideas, knowledge, expertise, and so on."[1]

Growing momentum

In years past, the Lone Ranger mentality in pursuit of a goal was the ideal for many ministries. In pioneer situations, in which there is much work to do but few people and agencies to do it, it has often been a necessity. But today partnership, or two or more organizations working together to achieve a common objective, is a growing reality in the evangelical missions movement.

Evidence of this can easily be found by comparing the subject index to missiologist David Hesselgrave's 1988 book on missions trends, *Today's Choices for Tomorrow's Mission*, and a copy of any current missions journal. The index makes no mention of the word "partnership"; the journal, however, will almost inevitably contain some discussion of partnership with nationals, Western agencies, or church to church.

Why has partnership become a trend in little more than a decade? Money is an ever-present consideration. (See chapters 2 and 3.) Partnering with nationals can make ministry cheaper, if it is done right. There are other reasons, too. As the church has become increasingly global, as technology has made cooperation more and more feasible, as Christians have become more sophisticated about the presence and gifts of overseas churches, and about mergers and strategic alliances in the business world, they are increasingly demanding that the agencies they support become involved in partnerships.

Paul Borthwick, a senior associate with Development Associates International, which is a ministry devoted to helping Third World leaders, says partnership with nationals is very much an issue in supposedly ethnocentric North American churches. "For the local church, thinking strategically means working with national leadership, at least in areas where the church is established," said Borthwick.

He quotes Cindy Judge of the Willow Creek Community Church as saying, "The mission-minded layperson has been hearing for years that missionaries are working themselves out of a job and empowering local leadership. We found that our laypeople expected it to be obvious to be working with nationals rather than missionaries from the US."[2]

In practice: partnership for the Balkans

The Northside Community Church in Atlanta has demonstrated partnership with nationals in its work in the Balkans. After reading Patrick Johnstone's *Operation World* prayer guide and statistical compendium, staff and members of the 400-member congregation realized that Yugoslavia was home to the least-evangelized Muslim group in Europe. In 1990 the church "adopted" the Bosnian Muslims for prayer. In 1992, according to John Siewert of the MARC *Mission Handbook*, the church began planning to send a short-term team to Sarajevo to start a church. However, civil war broke out, making the goal both more difficult and of greater urgency.

The church did some investigating and discovered a camp of 3,000 Bosnian refugees in Croatia. Also in that country, which had broken off from Yugoslavia, was the Evangelical Theological Seminary of Osijek, founded by Peter Kuzmic. The church formed a partnership with the school. Seminarians there became interpreters for Northside's church-planting teams. "Eventually," Siewert writes, "one-sixth of Northside Community Church's adults would become directly involved in Croatia."

By the time of the Dayton peace accord in November 1995, the ministry was well established with new disciples among the Bosnian refugees. Northside and Croatian churches began planting churches among the Bosnians returning home. Conversational English classes were added to supplement and expand the work, and the ministry now includes long-term missionaries as well. Other American churches, from the Arizona-based Antioch Network, have also joined the church-planting effort.[3]

Types of partnerships

While partnership most often refers to Western missionaries and non-Western nationals working one-on-one as equals, it can have a more structural meaning for missionary organizations. Agencies that cross ethnic or national lines to work together are said to be internationalized.

Four types of internationalized organizations are generally identified: (1) cooperative organizations, which share information informally, such as the Mission Advanced Research and Communication Center (MARC), publisher of many evangelization resources, including the *Mission Handbook*; (2) task-oriented organizations, spearheaded by groups such as Gospel for Asia and Interdev that bring several organizations together for a common goal; (3) international agencies such as WEC International and SIM, which operate in many nations or have multinational leaders; and (4) international movements in pursuit of a common goal or strategy, such as the Viva Network, World by Radio, and the AD2000 and Beyond Movement.[4]

Living partners

In 1999 the partnerships represented by the WEF (with national fellowships in more than 150 countries), the Lausanne Committee for World Evangelization (formed after the Billy Graham-initiated congress), and the AD2000 and Beyond Movement all agreed to join a still larger partnership. They have formed a global evangelization network called the Great Commission Global Roundtable. Members of the Roundtable's International Task Force come from Egypt, New Zealand, the Philippines, the USA, Australia, Brazil, Norway, Nigeria, Guatemala, and elsewhere. In the words of the WEF, "The Roundtable's purpose is to hear, serve and connect diverse segments of the Body of Christ in hopes of achieving closer coordination and cooperation in sharing the Gospel."[5]

Meanwhile, Global Mapping International (GMI), an agency devoted to providing maps and other research tools to help churches and other organizations break down the evangelistic task, is helping like-minded agencies around the world. For example, it is working with CAPRO, a Nigerian mobilization agency sending 350 missionaries throughout Africa. In November 1999, two GMI workers held a week-long training workshop in Nigeria to train leaders in mission research, mapping, and digital publishing. GMI is also helping the Korea Research Institute for Mission and is exploring partnerships in North and South India.[6]

On the direct ministry front, Interdev, which focuses on strategic evangelism partnerships, reports significant strides. The number of people in language groups with new evangelism and church-planting partnerships related to Interdev is more than 300 million. About 400 ministries from 50 countries now participate in these partnerships, many of which focus on the Islamic world. Nearly a third of the ministries involved are from the non-Western world. Interdev reports an 87 percent increase in the number of partnerships in one year.[7]

Partners International is perhaps the most respected and trusted Western agency promoting joint ministry with non-Western agencies. Partners does not disparage the work of Western missionaries (see chapter 2) but seeks to make the burgeoning non-Western force (see chapters 2 and 16) more effective through financial, organizational, and training help. According to Chuck Bennett, the former president, Partners supports more than 3,800 non-Western missionaries: "Over the past couple of years our 72 partner ministries in 50 countries have led an average of one

new person to Christ every 10 minutes and started a church in
an unchurched community every 11 hours. . . . Altogether, these
partner ministries work in at least 260 different people groups,
of which 161 are classified as 'unreached' peoples."[8]

The Arab world is another focus of ministry partnerships.
Besides Interdev's work, other partnerships there include Evangelicals for Middle East Understanding, which seeks to open
communication between Western and Middle Eastern Christians;
the Arab World Evangelical Ministers Association, a network
of Arab believers; and the Arabic Media Convention, a partnership using radio, television, and print. One of the media
partners, Middle East Media (MEM), says there is growing
interest in Christian materials in the Muslim world. MEM says
requests by ministry partners for its two openly evangelistic
booklets usually reach 20,000 annually. However, recent requests
added up to 130,000 copies in one year. As one source has
commented, "The consortium of agencies and churches working
cooperatively across North Africa and the Middle East is
increasingly finding a harvest field."[9]

Pitfalls of partnering

However, partnerships are not a panacea for world missions.
Paul Borthwick, who is also the head of the WEF's Youth
Commission, points out that the cooperation everyone expected
to flow from the 1974 Lausanne missions congress "has not
really been lived out" by the major players in the years since.[10]

Sometimes partnerships are just not possible. In some areas
there is no one to partner with, or, if there is, doctrinal differences
preclude cooperation. An unequal yoking of partners with
different strategic objectives (say, church planting and disaster
relief) can also cause friction.

With the best of intentions, usually accompanied by a lack of
cross-cultural understanding, partnerships can also collapse or
veer far off course. If the joint ministry is not perceived to be a
task among equals, financial and strategic paternalism can

emerge, with the Westerner calling the shots. Or the less powerful partner can become dependent on the largess of the stronger one. Some Christian leaders emigrate to the West, where life is easier. Others remain in their home countries, but the money they receive from Westerners separates them materially and emotionally from their flocks. To whom are they responsible? Who is footing the bill?

One common partnership problem that is little discussed occurs when Westerners bring African or other Christians from the Third World to study in the United States or Europe. The problem is not (always) the theological education received, but that many of the Two-Thirds World students decide to remain in the West when their schooling is over. The temptation to stay in more comfortable and affluent surroundings is simply too great, even though the primary needs are in their home countries. The issue is causing some wiser Western agencies to seek ways to provide education and ministry training "on the field."

One American teacher at a theological institution in Africa, fed up with the trend, has announced to his students that he will no longer provide recommendations for students wishing to study in America. He says "it is time for committed Christians to stop this tragic hemorrhage."[11]

Daniel Rickett of Partners International says ministries must help their ministry partners serve God through their own gifts and callings. The goal is not merely to do ministry together, but to develop one another in brotherhood: "In today's global village we have to learn how to deal with each other as true brothers and sisters, while learning to obey God and advance the gospel. This ultimately brings us to very practical questions about sharing power, resources, and responsibilities."[12]

FURTHER READING

"What local churches are saying to mission agencies," by Paul Borthwick, *EMQ*, July 1999.

"Preventing dependency: developmental partnering," by Daniel Rickett, *EMQ*, October 1998.

Partners in the Gospel, by James Kraakevik and Dotsey Welliver (Wheaton: Billy Graham Center, 1992).

"Growing local church initiatives," *Mission Handbook* (Monrovia: 1997).

Globalizing Missions, by David Hicks (Miami: Editorial Unilit, 1994).

Partnership: Accelerating Evangelism in the 90s, by Phill Butler, with Clyde Cowan (Seattle: Interdev, 1993).

Building Strategic Relationships: A Practical Guide to Partnering with Non-Western Missions, by Daniel Rickett (Pleasant Hill, Calif.: Klein Graphics, 2000).

DISCUSSION QUESTIONS

1. *What kinds of partnerships are being used in missions today?*

2. *What are some of the strengths and potential problems in this approach?*

3. *What elements make up a good partnership?*

4. *In what ways does your organization engage in partnerships?*

Chapter 12

Contextualization

While Paul was waiting for [Silas and Timothy] in Athens, he was greatly distressed to see that the city was full of idols. So he reasoned in the synagogue with the Jews and the God-fearing Greeks, as well as in the marketplace day by day with those who happened to be there. A group of Epicurean and Stoic philosophers began to dispute with him. Some of them began to ask, "What is this babbler trying to say?" Others remarked, "He seems to be advocating foreign gods." They said this because he was preaching the good news about Jesus and the resurrection. Then they took him and brought him to a meeting of the Areopagus, where they said to him, "May we know what this new teaching is that you are presenting? . . ."

Paul then stood up at the meeting of the Areopagus and said: "Men of Athens! I see that in every way you are very religious. For as I walked around and looked carefully at your objects of worship, I even found an altar with this inscription: 'To an Unknown God.' Now what you worship as something unknown I am going to proclaim to you.

"The God who made the world and everything in it is the Lord of heaven and earth and does not live in temples built by hands. And he is not served by human hands, as if he needed anything, because he himself gives all men life and breath and everything else. From one man he made every nation of men, that they should inhabit the whole earth; and he determined the times set for them and the exact places where they should live. God did this so that men would seek him and perhaps reach out for him and find him, though he is not far from each one of us. 'For in him we live and move and have

our being.' As some of your own poets have said, 'We are his offspring.'

"Therefore, since we are God's offspring, we should not think that the divine being is like gold or silver or stone – an image made by man's design and skill. In the past God overlooked such ignorance, but now he commands all people everywhere to repent. For he has set a day when he will judge the world with justice by the man he has appointed. He has given proof of this by raising him from the dead."

When they heard about the resurrection of the dead, some of them sneered, but others said, "We want to hear from you again on this subject." At that, Paul left the Council. A few men became followers of Paul and believed. Among them was Dionysius, a member of the Areopagus, also a woman named Damaris, and a number of others. – Acts 17:16–19, 22–34.

To the Jews I became like a Jew, to win the Jews. To those under the law I became like one under the law (though I myself am not under the law), so as to win those under the law. To those not having the law I became like one not having the law (though I am not free from God's law but am under Christ's law), so as to win those not having the law. To the weak I became weak, to win the weak. I have become all things to all men, so that by all possible means I might save some. I do all this for the sake of the gospel, that I may share in its blessings. – 1 Corinthians 9:20–23.

A tried and true approach

Contextualization may be a new term, but it is not a new concept. It has been around for as long as the Bible. Paul practiced it faithfully while preaching the gospel in Athens, and while living out the gospel before Jews and Gentiles, as the above passages demonstrate. Contextualization simply means finding points of contact within other people's contexts and removing things from one's own context that might block communication in order to gain a hearing for the gospel. It can be done verbally and nonverbally.

In Athens, Paul commended his audience's religiosity, carefully avoiding the use of the word "idols" when talking about their "objects of worship." He alluded to and quoted from their Epicurean and Stoic philosophers approvingly where he could. Then he filled their words with biblical content and corrected their errors; the unknown *theos* they worshipped was actually the sovereign and personal God of the Hebrew Scriptures. Rather than the Greek idea of the soul's immortality, Paul preached the resurrection, a new concept.

To the Corinthians, Paul, a Jew by birth, said he took on or removed the Jewish law according to the sensitivities of his hearers. For Jews who would be offended by his freedom, he submitted to the dietary and ceremonial strictures of the Old Testament so they would listen to his message of freedom in Christ. For Gentiles who would be put off by these regulations, Paul abandoned them, secure in his freedom, so that he could tell them about the moral requirements of God that Christ fulfilled.

Contextualization has been a hallmark of the modern missionary movement, too, from William Carey's translations of Hindu classics in India, to Hudson Taylor's decision to "go native" in China, to Bruce Olson's determination to become a member of the Motilone Indian tribe. It will continue to be a vital cross-cultural missionary approach in the 21st century, because continuing cultural differences in language, belief systems, and worldview will demand it.

Contextualization and culture

Culture, of course, is generally seen as a society's folkways, mores, language, art, and architecture, and political and economic structures; it is the expression of the society's worldview. Worldview has been described as the way a people looks upon itself and the universe, or the way it sees itself in relationship to all else. All worldviews, according to David Hesselgrave, have four main elements: mankind, nature, the supernatural, and time. Three archetypal worldviews are secularism, animism, and theism.

For the cross-cultural contexualizer, witness involves a thorough understanding of one's own culture, the biblical context in which God's word was given, and the culture of those one is evangelizing. The message must be tailored or contextualized in such a way as to remain faithful to the biblical text while understandable in and relevant to the receptor's context.

The late 20th century saw, along with widespread acceptance of anthropological insights, a flowering of respect for culture in missions and evangelism. At the 1974 Lausanne Congress on World Evangelization, Ralph Winter argued that 2.7 billion people cannot be won to Christ by near-neighbor evangelism since they have no Christian neighbors. Winter called on evangelists to cross cultural, language, and geographical barriers, learn the languages and cultures of these unreached peoples, present the gospel to them, and plant culturally relevant churches among them. Winter's emphasis on crossing cultural boundaries to reach other cultural groups laid the foundation for the unreached peoples movement and the AD2000 and Beyond Movement. It also gave a powerful boost to contextualization as a missionary method.[1]

At the 1978 Lausanne Committee consultation on Gospel and Culture, 33 missions leaders and theologians drafted *The Willowbank Report*, which set down a detailed acknowledgment of the critical role of culture in missionary communication. Included in the document were evangelical understandings of culture, Scripture, the content and communication of the gospel, witness among Muslims, a call for humility, and a look at conversion and culture. The authors asserted that conversion should not "de-culturize" a convert.[2]

As evangelical understanding of culture has progressed, a number of innovative evangelism methods have been advanced. Noting that the theology of the Bible is often encased in stories, Tom Steffen of Biola University and others argue that storytelling can be more effective in oral cultures than the Western-style cognitive teaching approach.[3] Baptists working among the

Muslim Kotokoli people of Togo have found that storytelling can lower cultural barriers to the gospel.[4] Use of Western forms of communication may also stigmatize the gospel as alien in some cultures. A cross-cultural approach advocated for shame cultures – some Islamic societies, for example – is to emphasize the gospel as the answer for defilement and uncleanness rather than sin and guilt.[5]

A new contextualization trend among missionaries is the use of indigenous music rather than imported Western words and styles. Drawing from the insights of ethnomusicology, missionaries are using local music forms to both strengthen new Christians in their faith and to reach out to unbelievers. The Summer Institute of Linguistics offers summer courses, an annual conference, and a library on the subject.[6]

Some critics have questioned the effectiveness of popular evangelism tools such as Evangelism Explosion when used apart from an adequate understanding of the culture and contextualization. Steffen argues that before the *Jesus* film is shown, the audience's worldview must be known, the presenters must earn the right to be heard, the film must be seen first by the community's information gatekeepers, the presenters must grasp how the community makes decisions and must know how to incorporate converts into healthy churches, and the audience must have a significant foundation for the gospel. Not to have these cultural prerequisites in place, he and others argue, is to invite nominalism or syncretism.[7]

Risk of syncretism

Syncretism, or the unbiblical blending of true religion with false, is an ever-present risk for the contextualizer. The key is to keep biblical elements that are non-negotiable and to discard unbiblical cultural or religious elements. Catholic missions in past centuries, in their zeal to bring masses of pagans into the church, sometimes failed this test, as the old gods were simply given new Christian names. In supposedly Catholic bastions from Mexico to the

Philippines to Haiti to Brazil, animistic practices survive under a Christian veneer.

Catholics are not the only ones facing the problem of syncretism due to faulty contextualization, of course. According to missiologist Ralph Winter, perhaps a third of the 6,000 churches linked with the African Independent Church movement are messianic, meaning they have someone among their members known as a divine person. Winter believes the Spirit and the Word, without Western intervention, will lead many of these churches into orthodoxy.[8] That is certainly debatable.

In the case of the AmaZioni Church of South Africa, however, missionaries are taking an active role in untangling the syncretism of the movement, whose name means "people of Zion." The church was started by missionaries in the early 1900s, but it had to grow on its own after internal and financial problems forced the Westerners to withdraw. Lacking qualified teachers, many AmaZioni groups became syncretistic, allowing for speaking with ancestors and frequent baptisms. One observer estimates that in a typical congregation, 20 percent of the people are evangelical, 20 percent follow tribal religions, and 60 percent are open to the direction of leaders.

Taking advantage of its historical ties with the AmaZioni, the Mahon Mission of Zion, Illinois, is sending missionary teachers to train local leaders to undo the decades of wrong doctrine by using the *Jesus* film, a correspondence course, and by helping church leaders receive seminary training.[9]

Another tricky issue in contextualization concerns India. Echoing the method of the 17th-century Jesuit priest Robert de Nobili, who donned Hindu garb to win converts, a Youth With A Mission team in North India is working with an Indian Christian. The man wears traditional robes befitting a *sadhu*, or holy man. He and the team organize pilgrimages to Hindu religious sites for pilgrims. Along the way, he and the missionaries explain the gospel "in a totally contextualized way. As far as the pilgrims are concerned, he is a Hindu. He's a Brahmin *sadhu*."[10]

Meanwhile, some Indian Christians say they are Hindus, or "Hindu Christians," reasoning that "Hindu" is sometimes a cultural rather than religious term that can mean no more than "Indian." Joseph D'Souza, who chairs the All India Christian Council, says Christians define "Hinduism" too broadly, even as a religious term: "What Christians have traditionally attacked represents large elements of classical Hinduism and Brahminism – such as God being impersonal, the caste system, etcetera," he said. "However, there are other systems that allow for a personalized, incarnated God. . . . (These) have become a great bridge builder to millions of people who are favorable and responsive to the gospel."[11]

Gary Corwin, a former missionary to Ghana and the editor of *Evangelical Missions Quarterly*, has noted the development of "super-contextualization," which he defines as "a new willingness to push the envelope of cultural and religious accommodation way beyond current practice."[12] Whether Hindu Christians fit this description is still anyone's guess, but new and sometimes troubling approaches to Muslims definitely qualify.

The special case of Muslims

Back in the 1970s, Phil Parshall was a missionary in an Asian Muslim country. Parshall and his team hoped to reach more Muslims by removing Western cultural impediments to the gospel, since the gospel is transcultural. They tried to create identifiable Christ-centered communities using religious language (such as "Allah" for God) and cultural and religious forms (such as kneeling, Muslim style, in prayer) permitted by the Bible. However, the converts were not encouraged to remain a part of the local Islamic mosque or to call themselves Muslims. God, Parshall says, "has greatly honored our efforts in that country."

Today, however, some missionaries have taken the approach a step or two farther. They encourage Muslims who receive Christ to continue to worship in the mosque and call themselves Muslims, since "Muslim" means (literally) one who is submitted to God. They reason that these "Muslims" will be better able to reach their friends and neighbors the longer they can remain in their communities. Some of these missionaries, but by no means all, even call themselves Muslims, in an attempt to "become a Muslim to reach the Muslims." They assert that Christ calls people to change their hearts, not their religions, and that a person can truly be classified a Muslim without believing every tenet of Islam, just as millions of people in the West are labeled Christians even though they know nothing of saving faith.[13]

Arguments against "becoming a Muslim"

But is it really possible to "become a Muslim to reach the Muslims"? Here are some brief arguments against this practice.

1. It is dishonest. Claiming to be a Muslim means, to Muslim ears, to submit to Allah (the Arabic word for "God") as revealed in Islam. This supposed deity is nothing like the covenant-keeping personal Lord of Scripture. Claiming to follow Allah while swearing allegiance to Jesus Christ is a deception Muslims would not appreciate. It is also deceptive to receive prayers and money from Christian churches while living as a Muslim "on the field."

2. Islam is an anti-Christian religious system. Claiming, as some missionaries do, to practice Islam but to love Jesus Christ is an untenable contradiction. Islam, which came into the world in the 7th century after Christ, says it is the final revelation of God, that the Christian Scriptures are corrupted, that Jesus did not die on the cross, that one must practice the Five Pillars of Islam, and that Muhammad is a prophet. Claiming to be a part of Islam and a part of Christ's church seems to come dangerously close to linking light with darkness.

3. Islam is not analogous to the Judaism of Paul's day. It is patently and consciously anti-Christian, as its history of restrictive or harsh dealings with Christians demonstrates. Paul could claim to be a Jew because he was born a Jew, and because Old Testament Judaism was part of God's

special revelation preparing the way for Christ. Islam can make no such claim.

4. Becoming a Muslim is not analogous to becoming a Gentile. Being a Gentile was a matter of ethnicity, not religion. When Paul spoke of becoming a Gentile to reach the Gentiles, he meant that he would avoid certain Jewish laws regarding food and other matters. Paul did not literally become a Gentile; he remained a Jew. Becoming a Muslim in the Pauline sense would certainly allow Christians to put aside certain cultural practices offensive to Muslim sensibilities. Paul did not say that he became a pagan to reach the pagans, however, so he was not talking about changing his religious identity.

5. Attending mosque or reading the Muslim holy book, the Qur'an, in the expectation of hearing from God forces the Christian believer into syncretism. In the mosque Muhammad is said to be God's prophet. The Qur'an claims to be the literal words of God. Christians cannot accept either of these claims and remain faithful to the Bible.

A study of a contextualized group in a region code-named Islampur reveals some of the dangers of syncretism. Members were allowed to worship in the mosque and read the Qur'an, in addition to learning from the New Testament and gathering together for worship. Leaders of the group, which has an estimated 45,000 converts, were surveyed for their religious practices and beliefs. Two-thirds maintained that the Qur'an was the greatest holy book; 45 percent did not affirm the Christian Trinity; and about a third went to the mosque more than once a day.[14]

Limits to contextualization

Yes, contextualization in general is good. Effective, culturally sensitive communication occurs in many cases, as Paul and others have demonstrated down through the centuries. Growing, healthy churches are able to reach their same-culture neighbors when they are not saddled with Western theological formulations and worship styles. A better expression of the richness of the church comes from biblical contextualization, which highlights the good and true in any culture while linking it to biblical truth. But, like anything else, when taken too far, contextualization can be toxic. Christians in the 21st century will need to carefully reflect on the Bible to know where to draw the line.

Contextualization is not a missionary silver bullet. An over-reliance on this method bespeaks an underreliance on the Holy Spirit, whose job it is to convict the world of sin, righteousness, and judgment, and to regenerate human hearts.

"One hundred percent contextualization is not going to guarantee belief," stated Dallas Theological Seminary's Michael Pocock, referring to reaching peoples deemed resistant to the gospel. "It's a spiritual dynamic. We don't want to be too Calvinistic about the thing, but somehow it's in God's hands."[15]

Sometimes contextualization is not even necessary. Contextualizing the gospel to reach the many Muslims in Nigeria and Iran who are disillusioned with their religion, for example, would be counterproductive. James Peterson of the Lutheran Orient Mission Society tells of receiving a phone call several years ago from a Kurdish woman claiming to be meeting with about 30 other women in the name of Jesus.

"Have you left Muhammad?" he asked her.

"Of course, Brother," she replied. "We need the gospel."[16]

FURTHER READING

"Danger! New directions in contextualization," by Phil Parshall, *EMQ*, October 1998.

"Crossing the music threshold," by David Nelson, *EMQ*, April 1999.

"His ways are not our ways," by Joshua Massey, *EMQ*, April 1999.

Cultural Anthropology: A Christian Perspective, by Stephen A. Grunlan and Marvin K. Mayers (Grand Rapids: Zondervan, 1979, 1988).

Communicating Christ Cross-Culturally: An Introduction to Missionary Communication, by David J. Hesselgrave (Grand Rapids: Zondervan, 1991).

Communicating Christ in Animistic Contexts, by Gailyn Van Rheenen (Grand Rapids: Baker Book House, 1991).

Bruchko, by Bruce Olson (Lake Mary: Creation House, 1978).

Inside the Community: Understanding Muslims Through Their Traditions, by Phil Parshall (Grand Rapids: Baker, 1994).

Missiology and the Social Sciences, edited by Edward Rommen and Gary Corwin (Pasadena: William Carey Library, 1996).

Muslims and Christians on the Emmaus Road, edited by Dudley Woodberry (Monrovia: MARC, 1989).

Contextualization: Meaning, Methods, and Models (Grand Rapids: Baker, 1989).

DISCUSSION QUESTIONS

1. *Define contextualization, syncretism, worldview, and culture.*

2. *When is contextualization good, and when is it bad?*

3. *Do you believe it is acceptable for people from Muslim communities to continue to attend a mosque and call themselves Muslims? What about missionaries? Support your answer from Scripture.*

4. *What are some of the benefits of contextualization?*

5. *What are some of the limits of contextualization?*

Chapter 13

Missions as Process vs. Missions as Project

In 1962, Kenneth Swain and five other members of a Christian and Missionary Alliance translation team arrived in Vietnam's central highlands to begin producing a Bible for the Raday people. During the Vietnam conflict, the Raday sided with the American military. The American soldiers eventually left, leaving the Raday and other peoples, like the better known Hmong, to face retribution at the hands of the communists.

The Raday Bible translation team also suffered. Most of them were killed by the communists, including missionary Robert Ziemer, who was shot dead during the Tet offensive in 1968. Swain, who was on a hit list, was on furlough. He is the only survivor of the original six.

Those Raday who could, left Vietnam. Yet the Bible translation work continued, year after year. In September 1999, the finished Bible was unveiled to the public. At three volumes and more than 1,700 pages, it would take a shopping cart to carry it all at once. Three congregations of refugees in North Carolina are benefiting, but the greater need is to get the Bible into the hands of their hard-pressed kin in Vietnam.

The need for the Raday Bible has never been greater. The tribal churches associated with the C&MA had only around 25,000 people during the 1970s. Today, among a population of 2 million people in the region, there are more than 100,000 believers.[1]

Without a long-term commitment to the task, through all the changes in personnel and venue, the Raday Bible never would have been completed. Such is the story of missions. Almost everything in missions history proves the adage, "Good things come to him who waits." Marvelous breakthroughs that seem so sudden have often been preceded by months and years of prayer, planning, and painstaking ministry.

A new approach

Yet much in today's missions scene seems at odds with this tried-and-true approach. Local churches and some of the newer agencies are sending out their own people, bypassing the traditional agencies in the name of better efficiency and stewardship (see chapter 1). They are expending great amounts of resources on the unreached peoples of the 10/40 Window, often to the exclusion of the traditional mission fields (chapter 7). They are supporting projects with defined, short-term goals (AD2000 and Beyond, World By 2000, the *Jesus* film, etc.; see chapter 8). They are using prayer not necessarily to discern and participate in God's will for the nations, but to break down demonic strongholds so that the gospel can be given to the spiritually blinded (chapter 9). They are sending more and more short-termers, while the long-term force continues to decline (chapter 10).

The long-term people at first tried to ignore this trend. Then they dismissed it. Now they are trying to work with it. Some are even trying to learn from it.

Two streams

David Dougherty, a member of the headquarters staff of OMF International since 1988 and a former church pastor, has thought deeply about these trends, and writes, "Such trends, among others, point to a significant division among mission mobilizers and strategists, perhaps one of the most important shifts since the end of World War II. The increased emphasis on the challenge of unreached peoples has highlighted two major streams of action: (1) *Missions as process*. This is the ongoing activity of traditional agencies, churches, and training institutions. They focus on fulfilling the Great Commission in every nation and among every people group. (2) *Missions as project*. This is the new outreach of mobilization organizations, churches, and individuals. They focus primarily on the unreached, or the least reached, people groups."[2]

Other parts of this book examine elements of the "missions as project" stream, but this chapter looks at the mindset itself. Dougherty says the newer group has been influenced by hordes of Christian baby boomers seeking to use their spiritual gifts and entrepreneurial know-how to renew their churches, by the establishment of tens of thousands of independent charismatic churches (chapter 17), by the spreading global church (chapters 2 and 16), and by the end of the millennium (chapter 8).

"The existing structures in the missions as process stream were not readily able to assimilate these new people and new ideas," Dougherty writes. "Therefore, at least two things happened: (1) new organizations sprang up to accommodate them; and (2) some churches started to see world missions as they saw the other ministries in the church, as something they should and can do themselves."[3]

Flexibility required

Indeed, in many churches and organizations the paradigm has shifted from the traditional long-term culture- and language-learning for church planting to short-term tasks, often involving novices. As might be expected, superficial ministry is sometimes a result of "project" missions. But the desire to get hands-on experience and use one's God-given entrepreneurial spirit for the kingdom can only be applauded. Anything that increases ownership of the Great Commission or excitement to complete it is at least going in the right direction and should be encouraged and channeled to productive uses. "Process" people, who know the missions ropes better, can help greatly in this. And they might even learn something in the process.

JAARS, the service arm of Wycliffe Bible Translators, the epitome of a long-term agency, recently added a ministry providing an outlet for church people who want to do projects.[4] It is just one of many. Paul Beals, professor emeritus at Grand Rapids Baptist Seminary, says agencies must find ways to incorporate these people, especially since their long-term recruits are in decline. "Mission agencies now find themselves serving an expanding group of people who want to serve in intercultural contexts," Beals writes. "With the explosion of short-term missions of many types, the agencies must find ways to oversee a variety of individuals and teams intent on making an impact for Christ."[5]

Long-term necessity

People in the project stream also need to be flexible, even if this means considering long-term service. They need to recognize that Christian missions is a 2,000-year-old process that likely won't be completed this week, or even this decade. Missions theorists and practitioners, such as Kevin Higgins among Muslims and David Bjork among secular Europeans, "stress the necessity of long-term, incarnational and vulnerable living in the host community."[6]

The massive CoMission project in the former Soviet Union is an example of the project stream beginning to merge with its process counterpart. The project aimed to introduce God's Word in the formerly atheistic empire, and as quickly as possible. From 1992 to 1996 the CoMission sent more than 1,500 volunteers into 2,500 schools in the region. Some 40,000 teachers and school administrators were introduced to a Bible-based curriculum in 131 two- to three-week convocations, and 50,800 copies of the *Jesus* film were given to teachers.

Despite all this, some in the missions movement wondered if there would be any long-term fruit from all this extensive sowing.

Perhaps in response to this concern, and to increasing government restrictions on religious activity perceived as foreign, the ministry has morphed into CoMission II, which has a church-planting emphasis. The approach now is to leave nationally led Bible discussion teams in each city where a CoMission team has served or a convocation has been held.

Peter Deyneka of Russian Ministries was named chairman of CoMission II. "As exciting as the first years of The CoMission have been, we now look ahead to a new time of partnership between CoMission teams and newly converted and seasoned Russian Christians," Deyneka said.[7]

MBMS International, a ministry of Mennonite Brethren churches in the USA and Canada, has long experience of sending short-termers into ministry. Now it has a team of young adults who have committed to serve together in Asia for at least ten years. "To make an impact long term requires learning the language and the culture," stated Andy Owen, a member of Team 2000. "Those things aren't going to happen in a one- or two-year term." MBMS's Dave Dyck adds, "We believe that the potential for sustained impact in their service setting is significant."[8]

FURTHER READING

"What's happening to missions mobilization?" by David Dougherty, *EMQ*, July 1998.

DISCUSSION QUESTIONS

1. *What are some of the reasons for the recent popularity of the "missions as project" approach to ministry?*

2. *What are the pros and cons of the "process" and "project" approaches?*

3. *What can "process" people learn from "project" people, and vice versa?*

4. *How might the two streams work together better?*

Chapter 14

Tentmaking

A few years ago, a Christian decided to do missionary work in a restricted-access country as a "tentmaker." However, authorities soon kicked him out after the government demanded evidence that he was actually engaging in the business specified on his visa. Since he viewed the job merely as his ticket into the country, he had no such evidence.

Later, this missionary returned to set up a legitimate small enterprise. But he also continued to receive money from churches and individuals as his primary means of support. A suspicious colleague in the country discovered that the Christian was really a missionary, thus generating even more resistance to him and his message.[1]

"Magic bullet" misfires

Tentmaking, or doing missionary ministry while working in a non-religious occupation, has become increasingly popular among Western missions agencies and churches. Self-supporting tentmakers, taking as their model the tentmaking apostle Paul in Acts 18:3, are said to be able to enter restricted access countries closed to traditional missionaries in the Muslim world and elsewhere. At the same time, they have been touted as able to bypass the difficult, time-consuming, and uncertain process of raising financial support from reluctant or overcommitted churches and individuals.

Too often in recent years, however, this missions "magic bullet" has misfired, sometimes hitting devoted supporters of the approach squarely in the foot. Between the boldface letters of hype, increasing numbers of astute observers in churches and missions agencies have become aware of tentmakers overseas wracked with guilt because of their double identity, or sent home broken and defeated thanks to a lack of training in spiritual or cross-cultural ministry, or an inability to balance the demands of their secular job with their spiritual ministry.

New maturity

Today the movement is gaining a new maturity that promises to allow it to fulfill some of its promises and complement the older, more established missions movement. "Ten years ago, tentmaking was a novelty," stated Ted Yamamori, president of Food for the Hungry, a relief and development agency, and a coordinator of the Tentmaker Track at the international Lausanne II missions congress in Manila in 1989. "Nowadays more people are talking about tentmaking. It's more organized, and networking is going on worldwide."[2] Indeed, in March 1994, 70 strategists from 17 nations met in the northern Thailand city of Chiang Mai to form the Tentmakers International Exchange (TIE), which had been planned since Lausanne II.[3]

"There is a strong and growing interest in tentmaking," said William Taylor, who heads the Missions Commission of the World Evangelical Fellowship, an international umbrella organization representing over 150 national evangelical groups. "The most common version in the West is the engineer or teacher serving in a restricted access country. This variety is seen in Asia particularly, less so in Africa and Latin America. But another category is the Filipino contract worker, and there are about 500,000 of these working in other countries. The Philippine Missionary Association has set the goal to train 2,000 evangelical contract workers as conscious tentmaking missionaries. This is a truly strategic and brave force that is particularly impacting the tough Muslim Arab nations."[4]

Christians from around the world are sticking their necks out in tentmaking roles. While employed by the National Conservatory of Music in Tetuan, Morocco, Salvadoran violinist and orchestra conductor Gilberto Orellana saw 14 Moroccan Muslims receive Christ during the two and a half years he and his family were in the "closed" North African state. Authorities eventually jailed Orellana, convicted him of proselytizing, and sentenced him to a year in prison before expelling him from the country.[5]

Kingdom professionals

Perhaps responding to the ethical quandaries faced by tentmakers who use the strategy merely as a means to enter otherwise closed countries, leaders of the US member of the TIE network, called Intent, advocate a broader understanding of the tentmaker role. Intent (formerly the US Association of Tentmakers) is a network of about 50 agencies and 100 to 120 individuals. Gary Ginter, a member of Intent's board, prefers the term "kingdom professional" to "tentmaker."

"We feel that tentmaking has come to be thought of primarily as a financial strategy, and we don't think that it is," Ginter said. "The issue is much more one of the people of God using the gifts of God . . . for the works of God. Tentmaking, properly understood, in our mind, is the marketplace ministry of effective Christians in cross-cultural contexts. And to the extent you move away from that, you begin to tread on thin ice."[6]

Mobilization efforts

Intent organizes conferences to spread its message and enhance the networking of tentmaker-minded mission leaders, churches, and strategists. "Within the next 10 or 15 years, the greatest percentage of people will be going out (as missionaries) in this way," asserted Carol Davis of Intent. "But there are very few agencies that are really open. Most of them have tried it and feel it doesn't work."[7]

WEC International's Jim Raymo is one mission executive who raises questions. Raymo, who wrote the 1997 book *Marching to a Different Drummer*, shared some of his concerns in an article in *Evangelical Missions Quarterly*. "Many unreached areas of the world cannot accommodate tentmakers, and tentmakers often have little time and energy to do evangelism and church planting anyway," he said.[8]

Actually, there are no comprehensive statistics showing how many tentmakers exist, not to mention success or failure rates. Universal agreement on the precise definition of tentmaking is elusive, as each group nurtures its favorite nuances. Nevertheless, interest in tentmaking by US Protestant agencies, although minor when compared to the traditional support-raising missionary, continues to grow. Yamamori, author of the 1993 book on the need for humanitarian tentmakers, *Penetrating Missions' Final Frontiers*, says the recent interest in the 10/40 Window (see chapter 7) "has really accentuated the need for tentmaking."[9]

According to the *Mission Handbook*, the number of US tentmakers has increased from 1,040 in 1992 to 3,220 in 1999. By contrast, the number of traditional cross-cultural missionaries (short- and long-term) declined from 50,550 to about 43,000 over the same period.[10] While the relatively few agencies that use tentmaking tend to view it as a supplemental rather than a primary strategy, openness to working with organizations such as Intent is on the rise.

"Frankly, as an organization, we keep trying to say, 'What's our niche?'" said Dave Brown of The Evangelical Alliance Mission (Wheaton, Illinois). "I think we're going to have to increasingly say, 'How can we partner? How can we set up these networks and work together?'"[11]

Skeletons in the desert

Brown added that many in the missions community still view tentmaking as "a financial ploy of people who don't have the guts to do deputation." They are also rightly concerned, he said, with "the skeletons lying out in the desert of people who have gone out there and they didn't know what they were doing and they weren't connected with anybody."[12]

Some of the strongest interest in the strategy comes from churches looking to unleash their laity for world missions in cost-effective and creative ways. To help them avoid some of the common pitfalls, in 1993 the World Evangelical Fellowship published a manual (since updated) for churches with tentmaking candidates, *Working Your Way to the Nations: A Guide to Effective Tentmaking*.[13]

Successful tentmaking models aren't lacking, even from established Christian organizations that make no secret of their presence in sensitive countries. Since 1954, the United Mission to Nepal has provided a plethora of humanitarian services in the name of Christ to the citizens of that poor, largely Hindu country, with the government's blessing. InterServe (founded in 1852 and based in Upper Darby, Pa.) has shifted from being what it calls a traditional mission to a tentmaking agency. Its unapologetically Christian workers use their secularly marketable skills in medicine, publishing, engineering, and the like in communities that need them, earning respect and the opportunity to share their faith further.

"Certainly, tentmakers are usually not going to build churches and equip other saints for ministry, but that is not necessarily their task in the overall scheme," stated Director Ralph Eckhardt. "Their responsibility is simply to witness, by word and deed, to people who have never been introduced to the gospel message before."[14]

New opportunities

The opportunities for tentmakers to have an impact have never been greater, according to Intent's Gary Ginter, as modernity and capitalism increasingly homogenize the cultures of the world. "One of the silver linings to modernity is it allows us an incredible range of ways to respond to cultures that we would otherwise be quite blocked out of," Ginter says. "[Tentmaking] is a supplemental strategy. It's by no means a panacea, but it is part of what I think God will use for the next 50 years."[15]

Wiser now, the Christian who was kicked out of the sensitive country now states, "Tentmaking is *not* an entry strategy. It is a lifestyle and a role one can choose to adopt for any number of reasons – only one of which should be the issue of access. But if chosen, the tentmaker better make, and sell, some tents."[16]

FURTHER READING

Working Your Way to the Nations, by Jonathan Lewis (Downers Grove: InterVarsity Press, 1997).

"Ministry, profits, and the schizophrenic tentmaker," by Steven L. Rundle, *EMQ*, July 2000.

DISCUSSION QUESTIONS

1. *Biblically, what is a "tentmaker"?*
2. *What are some of the reasons commonly given in support of this kind of ministry?*
3. *What are some of the ethical issues in tentmaking, and how can churches and agencies protect their integrity?*
4. *What are the differences between tentmaking as an access strategy, as a financial strategy, and as an expression of one's Christianity in the marketplace?*
5. *What kinds of tentmaking efforts does your group support? How could they be made more effective?*

Chapter 15

Holism

A proposed Southern Baptist plan to bring 100,000 "mission-aries" to Chicago in the summer of 2000 prompted a curious reply from area clergy. "While we are confident that your volunteers would come with entirely peaceful intentions, a campaign of the nature and scope you envision could contribute to a climate conducive to hate crimes," said a letter to Paige Patterson, president of the 15-million-member denomination.

Members of the protesting group said that they would be happy if the volunteers confined their work to public service projects. "We would welcome 200,000 people, if they were coming to improve the circumstances of life for Chicagoans who could use the assistance," one said to the *Chicago Tribune*. Another, however, said, "While this is coming in under the guise of good works, . . . it's clear that the agenda is to come and pursue converts."[1]

An old dilemma

Leaving aside the issue of whether sharing the gospel is itself a good work that will improve people's lives, the reaction above shows the suspicion verbal proclamation efforts receive, compared to works of service that are not explicitly tied to the gospel. This is not a new dilemma. While good works are almost always welcomed by everyone from secularists to Islamists, doing them in the name of Jesus is another matter, and proclaiming the message of the cross is another matter still. Peter and John were not hauled before the Sanhedrin because they healed a disabled beggar, but because they were preaching about Jesus. Peter boldly told the religious leaders, "If we are being called to account today for an act of kindness shown to a cripple and asked how he was healed, then know this, you and all the people of Israel: It is by the name of Jesus Christ of Nazareth, whom you crucified but whom God raised from the dead, that this man stands before you healed" (Acts 4:9–10).

Missionaries have almost always had some sort of social component to their evangelism and church-planting ministries, of course. Yet the pressure for Christians to do good works while keeping their mouths shut about Jesus was a hallmark of the 20th century. By the middle of the century, the World Council of Churches (WCC), under the influence of theological liberalism, had basically capitulated on the issue. Mission was defined not as preaching about the substitutionary death of Christ as payment for sins and the necessity of personal faith in him, but as doing a host of other good and worthwhile activities. At a 1968 WCC meeting in Uppsala, delegates decided to "let the world set the agenda."

Fueled by an uncertainty about the veracity of Scripture when it came to the lostness of people, these activities usually included everything but evangelism and church planting. Instead, civil rights, soup kitchens, even Marxist liberation theology were all subsumed under the category of "mission."

Christian reactions

Fundamentalists and, later, evangelicals, to their great credit, fought against these influences in the mainline churches. Some created new denominations, while others worked to reform decaying churches from within. However, the stigma of doing only evangelism in the face of the world's pressing needs spread. One reason was the civil rights movement of the 1960s. While some believers fought this good fight, others, either due to their own latent racism or faulty theology, remained on the sidelines.

Many Christians feared displacing evangelism and traditional missionary work from their priority perch as their liberal predecessors had done. Others sincerely believed a kind of modern Christian gnosticism, in which the world is viewed as simply a way station to heaven and not worth reforming, especially with the Apocalypse said to be coming soon. The main or only task of the church, as they saw it, was to rescue dying souls from a perishing world. But the civil rights movement encouraged some to rethink the role of evangelicals in society.

Another reason for the stigma attached to simply "spiritual" ministry was the spreading electronic communications revolution. Radio and television upended the way people saw and thought about the world. Crises such as tidal waves, earthquakes, and famine were beamed into living rooms on a nightly basis. Christians, their eyes opened to the needs of the world, could no longer claim ignorance. Many began looking into their Bibles again to find warrant for what the liberals termed social action. They began to say things like, "You can't just preach to a man who has an empty stomach."

A paradigm shift

The Lausanne Covenant, a major evangelical missiological document produced at the 1974 Lausanne Congress on World Evangelization, elevated social ministry as an important missionary task for Bible-believing Christians. "We affirm that evangelism and socio-political involvement are both part of our Christian duty," the Covenant affirmed. "For both are necessary expressions of our doctrines of God and man, our love for our neighbour and our obedience to Jesus Christ."[2]

In 1975 John Stott produced his paradigm-shifting book, *Christian Mission in the Modern World*. In it Stott said the defining statement of Jesus about missions is not the call to go and make disciples, found in Matthew 28:16–20, but John 17:18 and 20:21 ("As the Father has sent me, I am sending you"). To Stott, the call to mission is a call to do the works that Jesus did:

preaching the good news to the poor, proclaiming freedom for the prisoners and recovery of sight to the blind, releasing the oppressed (Luke 4:18–19).[3]

Evangelism and social action, according to Stott, are two sides of the same coin: "Neither is a means to the other, or even a manifestation of the other. For each is an end in itself." Elsewhere he said, "Mission describes ... everything the church is sent into the world to do."[4] For Stott this includes both development ministries and political involvement, a notion that has been adopted with zeal by both the religious right and left.

Proponents of this expanded definition of missions call it holism, or ministering to the needs of the whole person – physical, emotional, and spiritual. One of holism's most articulate spokesmen, Bryant Myers of the evangelical relief and development agency World Vision, states, "Holistic mission is a frame for mission that refuses the dichotomy between material and spiritual, between evangelism and social action, between loving God and loving neighbor."[5]

Examples of holism

Holistic mission goes far beyond soup kitchens. Microenterprise programs, inspired by the Grameen Bank of Bangladesh, encourage economic self-sufficiency among recipients through small revolving loans. One approach gathering momentum is the Samaritan Strategy, which aims to teach churches kingdom values, from a theistic framework, that promote development.

Darrow Miller of Food for the Hungry, in his 1998 book *Discipling Nations*, asserts that unbiblical worldviews, either secular or animistic, play a huge role in keeping people in poverty. By transforming people's thinking, Miller says, you can transform their circumstances. "All people and cultures have a particular model of the universe, or worldview," Miller says. "Their worldview does more to shape their prosperity or poverty, than does their physical environment or other circumstances."[6] From a missions perspective, the best holistic mission is done hand in hand with area churches, which understand local needs and are there to guide spiritual development.

A Peruvian cell group ministry through Food for the Hungry, an evangelical aid agency, began administrating health and income-generation programs in 1994. The groups addressed needs through Bible studies, social gatherings, and talks aimed at young people and newlyweds. Groups soon started in Peruvian churches.

Ted Yamamori, Food for the Hungry's president, says modern missions must emulate the first century church's combination of proclamation of the gospel and demonstration of the kingdom if it is to see a similar harvest. Yamamori says the traditional "harvesting" approach of missions is much less effective in the 10/40 Window than is the one he calls the "preparatory approach," which relies on acts of compassion to increase receptivity to the gospel.[7]

A force to be reckoned with

Holism is a force to be reckoned with in the new millennium, one that is unlikely to go away. "There is ample evidence from many corners today that whole communities (some of them very poor) are coming under the spell of Jesus, incarnated in his body, the church local, and are being transformed in part through the works and signs of Jesus manifest through ready, willing servants of the King and his kingdom," stated Steve Spaulding, Southeast Asia regional representative for Dawn Ministries in Manila, the Philippines. "In other words, there are at least enclaves which demonstrate the feasibility of broad-based transformation through the coming kingdom, mediated by the Spirit, the Word, and the Church, all to the greater glory of God. My inclination is to pray this kind of kingdom advance into ever wider circles of God's broken, fallen, disaster-ridden world."[8]

Jay Gary, director of the Christian Futures Network of Colorado Springs, sees transformation as the new missions paradigm in the 21st century. "The divide between evangelism and social action among evangelicals has been healed by a growing emphasis on community and national transformation," Gary said. "This model of ministry, or paradigm of how the kingdom comes, will likely supersede the Industrial Era models of 'evangelism' or 'discipleship.' Within five years we will see efforts by evangelicals to quantify the concept of 'transformation' with quality-of-life indicators. Whole new yardsticks will be used to measure the effectiveness of the church within a society or culture."[9]

An old danger

However, this emphasis on holism, as good as it is, carries a danger, which has been seen before in the ecumenical movement: the danger that traditional notions of evangelism and church planting will be neglected. One problem is the ever-present temptation to soft-pedal the preaching of the gospel in order to keep development programs and community relationships going. While advocates of holistic mission usually stress that evangelism and acts of compassion must work side by side, in practice this is not always possible.

One development professional says that transformation in a community depends on building relationships of trust. "These relationships, essential to many aspects of the development process, however, may depend upon incomplete transformation," stated World Relief's Meredith Long. "When a group of untouchables declare themselves as Christians or several Muslims declare themselves as followers of Christ, trust within the community often begins to dissipate, especially where conversion is a highly charged political issue. Christ recognized that the gospel would sometimes turn friends and family members against one another even when its presentation is done humbly and with sensitivity."[10]

Evangelical relief and development agencies have long had to battle the temptation to soft-pedal the gospel of salvation from sin, for a number of reasons. On the professional level, funds released by government agencies often come with strings attached that say none of it may be spent on evangelism. Or such outreach may be prohibited by the receiving country. There is also the subtle pressure to look respectable in the eyes of other development personnel, who work for secular groups. Also, some people who are not even evangelical in their beliefs may be employed by these agencies, because qualified evangelicals may not be available.

On the theological level, some development professionals in Christian agencies don't feel called to do evangelism, reasoning that their ministry is one of silent witness or "presence evangelism."

A 1991 survey uncovered a striking divergence of view on such matters between people who work for Christian relief and development agencies and the Christians who support them. By far the majority of Christians who contribute to these agencies see evangelism as their top priority. However, only 37 percent of agency staffers agree that "the ultimate goal of economic development projects should be to spread the gospel and convert people to Christian faith."[11] While ideally Christians should do both physical and spiritual ministry, sometimes priorities must be made. The priority of Jesus was not giving people physical bread but spiritual bread. When the crowds came to him clamoring for food, the Lord gave them a sermon instead (John 6).

Missiologist David Hesselgrave worries about the effects of the broader definition of mission. "There are strong indications that the 21st century will be marked by major sociopolitical upheavals and a succession of natural disasters," he said. "Unless this new – among evangelicals – understanding of mission is successfully challenged, the likelihood of retaining the biblical priority of world evangelization in the face of unprecedented needs of every kind will become increasingly difficult."[12]

FURTHER READING

"The missionary task: an introduction," by Arthur Glasser, in *Perspectives on the World Christian Movement: A Reader* (Pasadena: William Carey Library, 1992).

Christian Mission in the Modern World, by John Stott (Downers Grove: InterVarsity Press, 1975).

"Redefining holism," by David Hesselgrave, *EMQ*, July 1999.

"Another look at 'holistic mission,'" by Bryant Myers, *EMQ*, July 1999.

Discipling Nations: The Power of Truth to Transform Cultures, by Darrow Miller with Stan Guthrie (Seattle: YWAM, 1998).

DISCUSSION QUESTIONS

1. *Which is more important, pure evangelism or social action? Why?*

2. *In what ways does your church support ministries that do both?*

3. *What are some ways the two can be brought together?*

4. *What are some of the dangers in engaging in social ministry?*

5. *What are the strengths and weaknesses of the scriptural case presented for holistic mission?*

Part III

THE OVERSEAS CHURCH ARENA

Chapter 16

The Globalization of Christianity

Starting in April 1994, Rwanda took a machete to the hopeful, humanistic notion that people are basically good. Over the terrible months of spring and summer, an estimated 500,000 to a million Tutsis were hacked to death in the genocidal fury of their Hutu neighbors. This was not a regrettable blood-letting by pagan tribes, but a massacre carried out by at least nominal Christians. Some 80 percent of the tiny nation calls itself Christian, and the missionary presence has been significant through the years.

At the request of the Association of Evangelicals in Africa, Canadian Reg Reimer of the World Evangelical Fellowship's Department of Church and Society spent three months in the country gathering facts and working on a joint response. In December 1994, Reimer and leading African evangelicals managed to pull together 40 Rwandan church leaders scattered in the surrounding nations for a retreat in Nairobi. Leaders were challenged to build a new Rwanda.

Reimer has also conducted a workshop on reconciliation among Christians from Cambodia, Laos, and Vietnam. "They are developing some links among countries that have been at odds with each other and were used against each other in the Vietnam War," Reimer says. "That's a very significant development."[1]

Such international evangelical gatherings of mature Christian leaders would not have been possible even 40 years ago. The globalization of the gospel has been remarkable in the 20th century, particularly in the latter half. In 1960, an estimated 58 percent of the world's Christians were Westerners; in 1990, just

38 percent were.[2] Latin America's evangelical presence has exploded from a mere 200,000 or 300,000 in 1900 to tens of millions.[3] Today, about one-third of the earth's approximately 6 billion people are Christians at least in name. They are present in nearly every nation state. Most of the growth is coming in the former mission fields of Asia, Africa, and Latin America. From 1960 to 1990, the number of evangelicals in the West grew from 57.7 million to 95.9 million, while evangelicals outside the West multiplied from 29 million to 208 million.[4]

The shift was much in evidence at the New World Mission Congress for the Third Millennium, held 25–31 October 1999, in Kyoto, Japan. Of the 2,830 delegates at the Japan-organized gathering, some 2,500 were from Japan, with 330 from other nations. Overall, 120 nations were represented, including 108 from the so-called Third World.

In a keynote address, David Cho of South Korea noted that over the last four decades new forces for mission have emerged from the churches in Asia, Africa, and Latin America. Cho, founding chairman of the Third World Mission Association, said that "old orders of the world mission from the West [have been] reshaped into the global structure [that is] transnational, transcontinental, and multiracial." Cho said the congress was meant to prepare the way for "this new highway of missions for the coming new millennium."[5]

Biblical overview

In the Bible God anticipates and commands the globalization, or worldwide spread, of biblical faith. In the Old Testament, God blesses Abraham and promises that "all peoples on earth will be blessed through you" (Gen. 12:3). The people of God are told to "Declare his glory among the nations, his marvelous deeds among all peoples" (Ps. 96:3). The covenant community is open not just to Jews but to all who will follow Yahweh, such as Ruth of Moab. God's grace and compassion reach even the wicked people of Ninevah through Jonah and Naaman the Syrian through Elisha (2 Kgs. 5). The Servant of the Lord, fully realized in Christ, is to be "a light for the Gentiles, that you may bring my salvation to the ends of the earth" (Isa. 49:6).

In the New Testament, Jesus Christ tells the disciples, "And this gospel of the kingdom will be preached in the whole world as a testimony to all nations, and then the end will come" (Matt. 24:14). After the Resurrection, he commissions them to reach beyond the Jews and "go and make disciples of all nations" (Matt. 28:19). Just before his Ascension the Lord told them, "But you will receive power when the Holy Spirit comes on you; and you will be my witnesses in Jerusalem, and in all Judea and Samaria, and to the ends of the earth" (Acts 1:8). Acts chronicles the beginning of this expansion. The Bible assures us that at the end of history there will be "a great multitude that no one could count, from every nation, tribe, people and language, standing before and in front of the Lamb" (Rev. 7:9).

Historical overview

Christianity advanced unevenly around the globe during most of its first twenty centuries, with the church slow to remember its evangelistic mandate and all too quick to forget. However, despite occasional periods of persecution prior to A.D. 313, when Constantine issued the Edict of Milan, the church exploded across the Roman Empire. For the next three centuries, the Christian faith continued to spread through monks and bishops into Ethiopia, India, Ireland, and Britain, and along the trade routes toward Central Asia. In many areas, however, the church was weak from internal divisions and a failure to indigenize.

The coming of Islam brought a series of reverses from which the church has yet to recover. Lost to the Muslim invaders were the holy lands, North Africa, Asia Minor, and Persia. The Crusades did little to regain the lost territory, but much to stir up hatred and distrust among Muslims, feelings that persist to this day. The church, however, continued to spread across Europe, to what are now Belgium, Germany, and the Netherlands. Russia also became Christianized. Nestorian Christianity made its way into China but did not last. Later, the Dominicans and Franciscans brought Christianity to central Asia and China.

The church was firmly, and mainly, established in Europe when Martin Luther posted his 95 Theses in 1517. The Protestants, in a period of consolidation after the Reformation, did little outreach. The Catholics, aided by the great seafaring powers of Spain and Portugal, did much. The Jesuits entered many new areas, including South America. Protestants, inspired by the example of David Brainerd among the Indians of the New World and the Moravians of Germany, began to remember their missionary responsibilities.

But not until 1792, with the spark provided by William Carey, did the Protestant church begin vigorous outreach to other lands. The 1800s, sometimes called the great century of missions, saw the proliferation of missionary societies. Aided by the expansion of the great colonial powers, missionaries spread primarily from Europe and the United States to India, China, and Africa.

The selfless zeal of many of these missionaries often overshadowed the mistakes they made. Adlai Stevenson visited Africa during the 1950s. When asked what had most impressed him, he remarked, "The graves. The graves. At every mission station there were graves."[6]

But two world wars and the spread of communism in Russia and China put a damper on the church's optimism that the missionary task would soon be completed. After World War II, however, a new force of missionaries was created from those who had seen other parts of the world while they were soldiers. Their efforts, and the work of the churches and agencies they planted, laid the foundation for making Christianity the truly global faith it is today.

International missions force

As Christians in the countries that used to receive missionaries have realized their responsibility to be senders, too, the globalization of the missionary enterprise has begun to track the globalization of the church. The number of Protestant missionaries from the USA and Canada has declined, from 50,500 in 1988 to about 43,000 in 1999, according to the *Mission Handbook*.[7] South Korea and India each boast 4,000 missionaries, and the numbers continue to grow. Nigeria's Evangelical Missionary Society fields about 1,000 missionaries.[8] While the precise figures are disputable, the numbers of non-Western missionaries are certainly growing substantially faster than their Western counterparts. Some experts believe that Western missionaries have already been numerically eclipsed at the turn of the century.

Serious weaknesses

Hopeful Christian notions of the noble non-Western Christian are as off the mark as humanistic ones about the goodness of human nature. William Taylor, director of the Missions Commission of the World Evangelical Fellowship, warns against "unreal reporting and prognostications" regarding the non-Western missions movement. He says that Westerners generally have much more field experience. Taylor, formerly a missionary in Guatemala, dismisses the idealistic notion that non-Western believers are "the movement truly blessed by God," without warts. "There are serious weaknesses that must be addressed rapidly and seriously."[9]

While the day of Western missionary dominance is probably over, both raw need around the world and the biblical mandate to all Christians to spread the gospel ensure that Westerners will continue to have a job to do in world evangelization in the future, but perhaps more as partners, and less as leaders.

Alex Araujo, a Brazilian-born missions executive, adds, "Westerners need, most of all, to get used to the idea that they are not the only ones who can do the job well."[10]

FURTHER READING

"Reviewing the place of Western missionaries for the third millennium," by Donald K. Smith, *EMQ*, January 1999.

"Looking under the hood of the non-Western missions movement," by Stan Guthrie, *EMQ*, January 1995.

We Are the World: Globalization and the Changing Face of Missions, by J. David Lundy (Carlisle: OM Publishing, 1999).

Transforming Mission, by David J. Bosch (Maryknoll: Orbis, 1991).

DISCUSSION QUESTIONS

1. *In what ways is your church or agency responding to the globalization of the church and missions force? How are its ministries different than they were 10 years ago?*

2. *When was the last time your church yielded its pulpit to a qualified visiting non-Western leader?*

3. *How has the globalization of the church affected your view of the missionary task?*

4. *How do you feel about non-Westerners evangelizing in your country?*

Chapter 17

The Charismatic Boom

A typical Latin American Pentecostal service takes place in a large, poorly decorated meeting hall, with a full-blown band leading the singing, shouting, whistling, clapping, and dancing. As the service begins, the congregants become deeply immersed, their eyes closed, some crying, others singing at the top of their voice or "speaking in tongues," and still others lifting faces and hands toward heaven. The music goes on and on, building from soft strains to a fast, arresting rhythm that after nearly two hours reaches a deafening climax – and suddenly drops back again to quiet strains.

With the entrance of the pastor, the whole congregation shouts and claps, while he begins to preach a simple message of salvation in Jesus: You must convert now, while there is still time. No more drinking, cheating, and lying. The Lord is coming, soon. The music softly restarts while the pastor asks all who want to "accept the Lord" to come forward. As the leaders pray, the people start falling down – "slain in the Spirit," the outward expression of the Holy Spirit come into their lives.

There is no clear beginning of the service, and usually no clear end. Some because they have found what they prayed for, and others out of sheer exhaustion, begin to drift from the hall, and the service comes to an end. Nothing short of the final Rapture for which they pray will keep them from coming back next week, with friends and family in tow.[1]

Two-thirds of Latin America's approximately 60 million evangelicals are Pentecostal or charismatic. A powerful force for evangelism and missions, they constitute a full 40 percent of the world's charismatic population.[2] Meanwhile, the world's Pentecostals, a subset of evangelicalism, are growing at an 8.1 percent annual rate, 50 percent higher than the evangelical rate of 5.4 percent.[3] The Pentecostal community, including charismatics from many denominations, has gone from basically zero a century ago to 523 million today,[4] a sizable percentage of the 2 billion people who call themselves Christians world-wide.[5]

Therefore, any survey of the evangelical world missions movement that overlooks Pentecostals and charismatics is out of bounds from the start. As speaker and author David Shibley has said so well, "World evangelization can never be accomplished by charismatics alone. Neither can it be accomplished without us."[6] With that in mind, we will examine this flourishing movement to see what opportunities and dangers are ahead in the 21st century.

Roots of the movement

The number of Pentecostal Christians in the world would suggest that Pentecostalism has been around for centuries. The truth is, modern Pentecostalism is only about a century old. Some scholars trace its beginnings to 1 January 1901, when Agnes Ozman spoke in tongues in Topeka, Kansas,[7] others to the Azusa Street phenomenon in Los Angeles from 1906 to 1909, or to a schoolhouse in Murphy, North Carolina, in 1896.[8]

The first Pentecostals, looking back to the day of Pentecost when the Holy Spirit was given to the church (Acts 2), believed that all the gifts of the Spirit remain operative for the church today. These gifts include, but are not limited to, speaking in tongues and works of supernatural healing. While the early Pentecostals sprang from the holiness movement and formed their own denominations, since the 1960s the charismatic movement has touched nearly every strain of Christendom, including the mainline churches and the Catholic Church. In fact, Catholic charismatics form the largest subset within the American Pentecostal movement.[9]

Meanwhile, the Yoido Full Gospel Church, with 255,000 worshippers and 25,000 cell groups in Seoul, South Korea, is reputed to be the world's largest church. Another large charismatic cell church, according to Christian and Missionary Alliance missionary researcher Joel Comiskey, is the International Charismatic Mission of Bogota, Colombia. It has 45,000 worshippers and 24,000 cells.[10]

Empowered for witness

Far from being simply a navel-gazing, inward-focused religious experience, Pentecostalism has, from its inception, looked at spiritual gifts as the means for God's people to be able to do God's work. "Under the influence of the revivals that occurred in Keswick, England, Pentecostals viewed holiness not as an end in itself but as a preparation for empowered global witness," states Frank D. Macchia. "It was thought that in these latter days the Spirit would grant the people of God the apostolic capacity revealed in Acts 2:4 to proclaim the mighty deeds of God in the many languages of the world. Tongues were thought, therefore, to be the most striking evidence of a Spirit baptismal experience that urged one to bear witness of the gospel of Jesus Christ to the nations. Tongues were the primary evidence because Spirit baptism itself was viewed as an experience that thrust one into the challenges of a global witness that transcended established cultural boundaries."[11]

Pentecostals appeal to people around the world in part because their theology and practice speak to felt needs. Sometimes their efforts have been as simple as extending helping hands to homeless alcoholics or jobless laborers, who suddenly discover people who care and thus find a reason to live. Other efforts have been more organized. In Sabinópolis, a town in Brazil's central state of Minas Gerais, missionaries helped the Evangelical Missionary Pentecostal Church start a ministry called Bem Estar do Menar (Child Well-being). The ministry now provides child-care centers and educational, farming, and health programs. Not only have the lives of the area's poor improved, but since 1973, the church has grown from five to eleven congregations and from 200 to 2,000 adult members. [12]

A religion of the poor

From the beginning Pentecostal theology and practice have appealed, even in the estimation of critics, to the poor. "The movement that ensued was ridiculed by many outsiders as the religion of the economically deprived, the socially disinherited, the psychologically abnormal and the theologically aberrant," H. D. Hunter reports.[13] In Latin America, Pentecostalism continues to attract the poor. Peruvian theologian Samuel Escobar, a Baptist, has stated, "Today the churches that are growing in Latin America are Pentecostal churches, which grow among the urban poor."[14]

In the last two decades, the overall Latin Protestant church has about tripled in size. Some observers have speculated that this heralds radical change in the region, and not just in religion. In Brazil, Guatemala, and Nicaragua, for example, Protestantism is said to be the most widely practiced faith, surpassing the traditional Roman Catholicism.[15] There are many reasons for the allure. Latin Pentecostals are generally credited with encouraging hard work, with elevating women to leadership roles, and with breaking down some social and ethnic divisions.

"The significance of this goes beyond theology," John Marcom, Jr., wrote in *Forbes* a decade ago. "Upwardly striving urban poor are encouraged by religious teachings and support groups that preach the power of individuals to change their lives through faith. This contrasts sharply with the old attitude of resignation to one's fate and a glorification of poverty. The potential is quite literally revolutionary – more so than Fidel Castro or Che Guevara could ever be."[16]

Potential problems

Yet there is another side to the story, one that has applications beyond Latin America. Pedro Moreno, a Pentecostal lawyer from Bolivia who now works with Prison Fellowship, questions Pentecostalism's potential to transform Latin America. "The often assumed correlation of the rise of Evangelicalism in Latin America with socioeconomic development is certainly questionable," he said. "In fact, further Pentecostal contributions to social change are being hindered by Latin American Pentecostals themselves, specifically in three ways: with a line drawn too sharply between the religious and the secular, with an unnecessary rejection of reason in favor of emotion, and with a theological overemphasis on the 'call to ministry' and the end of the world."[17]

Latin Pentecostalism has, like many other religious movements, struggled to transcend some of its culture's deep-seated problems. One is the tendency to elevate strong leaders (*caudillos*) almost to demigod status. This can lead to theological error, or to hierarchies as bad as any found in the region's traditional Catholic religion.

Another problem is the risk of superstition spilling into the church. In parts of the region, of course, what is called Roman Catholicism is often a syncretistic mix with the animistic beliefs of bygone centuries. Unfortunately, the Pentecostal churches, with their emphasis on the supernatural side of faith, can easily fall into the same trap. "There's a fine line between what is supernatural and what is superstitious," states Ron Blue, president of CAM International, a noncharismatic mission formerly known as Central American Mission. "I'm not sure anyone can draw that line with accuracy."[18]

Indeed, it appears that Catholicism in Latin America is incorporating charismatic Christianity in much the same way it has in North America. People thirsting for more intimate and powerful experiences of the Spirit are, increasingly, staying in the Catholic church to get them. According to David Barrett, the proportions of Catholics (74 percent) and Protestants

(13 percent) in Latin America are stabilizing. "Is Latin America turning Protestant?" Barrett asks. "No, and it probably will not."[19]

And even the growth may not be all it's cracked up to be. Some reports hint that as many people are exiting Protestant churches through the back doors as are entering through the front doors. In Brazil, a recent survey by the Latin American Evangelism Service found that the number of "evangelical believers" is just 19.5 million, or half of what the most optimistic projections assert.[20]

Broadening theology?

Some of Pentecostalism's greatest theological strengths are also its greatest weaknesses. Its familiarity with the supernatural can lead to an unhealthy focus on evil (see chapter 9). Its evangelistic fervor, so critical in its growth and its burgeoning missions commitment, also encourages apathy about other issues in society – politics, relief and development, business, and so on. Many pastors have little regard for theological training, seeing it as unnecessary in Spirit-empowered witness. (Besides, many are so busy doing outreach that they have no time for it.) The fervor with which some Pentecostals await the "end times" is contagious, bringing a sense of expectation and purpose to lives mired in this world's poverty and degradation. Yet specific ministries to these needs, unless specifically directed through churches, are too often seen as second-tier, more worldly pursuits. Emphases on healing, tongues, and prophetic utterances, while responding to real needs and desires, are too often inner-directed.

Some observers believe that for Pentecostals and charismatics to make a greater difference, not only in eternity but also in time, they must recover and develop some theological themes latent in their movement. Frank Macchia, associate professor of theology at Southeastern College of the Assemblies of God, Lakeland, Florida, says that the apocalypticism of the early Pentecostals allowed them to stand outside of their culture and prophetically critique it. Now he wants them to take the next step and begin to transform it.

"Perhaps the most significant paradigm shift for Pentecostal theology as Pentecostals approach the 21st century will be to realize concretely something of the implicit ecumenical and multicultural witness of Pentecostals for the kingdom of God in the world," he said. "Such a realization will be shaped as much by voices from among the people of God as by voices from the world that point to urgent issues of global significance."[21]

FURTHER READING

"Pentecostals redefine religion in Latin America," by Pedro C. Moreno, *Wall Street Journal*, 29 August 1997.

"Hour of power: Latin America's Pentecostals are multiplying, as are questions," by Deann Alford, *World Pulse*, 1 October 1999.

The Globalization of Pentecostalism: A Religion Made To Travel, edited by Murray W. Dempster, Byron D. Klaus, and Douglas Peterson (Oxford: Regnum Books International, 1999).

The Holy Spirit and Mission Dynamics, edited by C. Douglas McConnell (Pasadena: William Carey Library, 1997).

Missions in the Age of the Spirit, by John V. York (Springfield: Logion Press, 2000).

DISCUSSION QUESTIONS

1. *What are the strengths and weaknesses of Pentecostal theology?*

2. *How might Pentecostals and other evangelicals learn to work together more effectively?*

3. *What are some of the dangers facing Pentecostalism in the 21st century?*

4. *Do you agree that Pentecostals need to take a more holistic approach to faith? Why or why not?*

Chapter 18

The Maturing of International Missionary Movements

Nsabimana Johnson, a member of the Tutsi tribe in Burundi, had turned his life over to Jesus when he was a young man. But civil war came to the tiny country in 1993, and Johnson's parents and relatives were killed by Hutus, a rival ethnic group. The next year, Hutus in neighboring Rwanda killed at least 500,000 people, mostly Tutsis. Many of the victims were cut down in churches.

"I was full of hatred against every Hutu person," Johnson said. "I didn't want to talk again with a Hutu or be reconciled with them."

Yet Johnson remained active in church, carrying his burden of hatred. Eventually he attended a retreat sponsored by the Minnesota-based Rouner Center for Reconciliation and supported by evangelical broadcaster Trans World Radio. At the retreat he came face to face with Hutu Christians. Guided by counselors, Johnson and the Hutus prayed, studied the Bible together, and began to see one another as real people.

"By the Word of God and by the Holy Spirit, I was touched in my heart, and I knew that if I didn't forgive those who had killed my family, I would never be free and happy in my life." He stood and sought forgiveness for his hatred.

"Now, I am free," he added, "and I love everybody without discrimination."[1]

Seeking an impact

Unfortunately, stories such as this one are too unusual in overseas churches. Nominalism, a curse in which people claim to be Christian but fail to act like it, has plagued much of the worldwide church. While the evangelical growth around the world could be characterized as a mile wide, too often it is no more than an inch deep. Nor is this simply a Third World problem.

Addressing 400 Christian leaders from 90 organizations and 54 countries, British evangelical churchman John R. W. Stott said at the September 1999 International Consultation on Discipleship that many parts of the global church are characterized by superficiality. "In some places the church is growing strongly, but even there the problem is that of growth without depth," he said. "In short, the church lacks proper discipleship."[2]

If discipleship means being able to live for Christ in the world but not of it, Stott has a point. Pedro Moreno offers the example of Latin America. "In Latin America there is a great religious revival, but it's not having a social, economic, or political impact," Moreno said. "It's mostly a religious phenomenon at this point. It's not changing the laws or the structures or the mentality."[3] Moreno says that Christians must learn to "externalize" their revivals into the larger societies around them if they are to allay suspicion and paranoia about evangelicalism (see previous chapter).

Africa, perhaps the most "Christian" of any continent, is too often mired in poverty, tribal hatreds, AIDS, and corrupt governments. "Where are the millions of Christians?" asked David Zac Niringiye, a Ugandan leader of the International Fellowship of Evangelical Students, to which InterVarsity Christian Fellowship belongs. "They are in business, politics, medicine, but how come there is no impact?"[4]

While not all of Africa's woes can be blamed on its churches, increasing numbers of Christians are seeking to be not just light but salt, too. In Uganda, the regional body of the International Fellowship of Evangelical Students has worked with the Kampala

Evangelical School of Theology to launch an Institute for Christian Impact. The institute offers seminars on social action, Bible exposition, democracy, politics, and the environment. At its inauguration, papers were presented on the themes of Christianity and culture, poverty, ethnicity, and environmental degradation. Speaking at the dedication, Stott said, "One of the most important questions facing Christians in every age and every place is, 'What values and standards are going to dominate our national culture?'"[5]

Making disciples

Committed disciples, not just converts, will be the ones in position to shape cultures in the 21st century. This was recognized at the International Leaders for Discipleship (ILD) meeting, where delegates signed a Joint Statement on Discipleship that stressed the following points: preaching the gospel and making disciples in all nations; acknowledging the local church's key role in making disciples; and not diluting the cost of following Jesus to make converts.[6] In addition, seven regional groups attempted to define what discipleship should be in their context in the 21st century. This discussion led a group of pastors and other leaders from Latin America to form CLADIS (Consulta Latinoamericana de Discipulado) in an attempt to deepen their impact. Mexican journalist Sally Ramirez, one of the founders of CLADIS, reports, "We've commissioned somebody to do a study on the state of discipleship in this area, and we're also working on a document that would give us a Latin American perspective on the biblical and theological basis for discipleship."[7]

Paul Borthwick, who works with a leader training agency, says discipleship is key to completing the Great Commission. "Make disciples, not converts," he advises. "We have emphasized the making of evangelical-experience converts, which has at times resulted in an anemic church and nominal disciples. We need to take Jesus' command seriously – making wholistic disciples rather than presenting a cheap gospel which implies that 'praying a prayer' is all it takes to be a follower of Christ."[8]

Tough critiques

Another sign of the maturing international missionary movement is the freedom of more and more non-Western ministry leaders to honestly criticize fellow-believers in the West. An example of this comes from India, where comments about Hinduism being demonic that had been published years earlier in the Pasadena-based *Mission Frontiers* magazine were picked up by national news media in India and roused a storm of controversy around the Christian minority. Unfortunate, and possibly triumphalistic, statements about Christianity in India were also posted on an AD2000 Web site. Such comments by evangelicals about Hinduism are nothing new, but the response of Indian Christians certainly was.

Joseph D'Souza, chair of the All India Christian Council, pointedly asked AD2000 leaders to help put an end to the incendiary rhetoric that was fueling a "huge propaganda war" against Christians. D'Souza also faulted some Indian Christian leaders influenced by the AD2000 Movement for "bombastic slogans, militant language and a general demeaning of Indian culture." Later, the India Missions Association and the National Council of Churches in India circulated a letter asking evangelistic agencies and networks to remove inflammatory material from their Web sites. The authors promised joint action if this were not done.

D'Souza is calling for accountability. "The time has come for the global evangelical community to act," D'Souza said. "At least the major players have to move seriously to bring a halt to all this destructive verbiage that is flowing on the Internet and other communication [media]."[9]

As the overseas missions movement gains confidence, it is increasingly realizing that brothers and sisters from the West do not have all the answers in world evangelization. And its spokesmen are becoming more and more likely to say so. At the consultation on evangelical missiology held in Iguassu, Brazil, during October 1999, Peruvian theologian Samuel Escobar fired a shot across the bow of certain segments of the Western missions corps. Escobar, who teaches at Eastern Baptist Theological Seminary, said that some church-growth groups have yielded to the spirit of the age by presenting missions as a "manageable enterprise," heavily dependent on statistics. Escobar called this approach "anti-theological," pointing out that it "has no theological or pastoral resources to cope with the suffering and persecution . . . because it is geared to provide . . . guaranteed success."[10]

The consultation, organized by the Missions Commission of the World Evangelical Fellowship, brought together 159 missiologists, executives, and missionaries from 53 countries. Most participants were from outside the West. The document they produced, the Iguassu Affirmation, reflects the diverse voices present. It declares at one point, "The insights of every part of the church are needed and challenges encountered in every land must be addressed. Only thus can our missiology develop the richness and texture reflected in the Scriptures and needed for full obedience to our risen Lord. We commit ourselves to give voice to all segments of the global church in developing and implementing our missiology."[11]

D'Souza has yet another criticism of Westerners. He says the Western practice of sending young, unmarried missionaries, either Western or non-Western, to certain parts of Asia is fundamentally flawed. He argues that more mature and seasoned family heads will be far more likely to get a hearing – if they can be recruited and retained. Younger workers, however, may play a role in making formerly open groups hostile to the gospel, particularly among Hindus and Muslims.

"We need to review how we recruit and send national workers," D'Souza says. "Young, single missionaries are good for presenting, proclaiming and informing people about the good news. They can also help where indigenous church planting and church-growth movements are already taking place. But they are ill-equipped to break new ground. They are ill-suited to bring long-term change in any social group."[12]

Seeking maturity

The US Center for World Mission in Pasadena estimates there are 2 million pastors in Asia, Africa, the Caribbean and Latin America, and the South Pacific.[13] Seeing Christian leaders overseas become mature in their faith and knowledgeable about the Word is a pressing goal of organizations as diverse as Development Associates International, Peter Deyneka Russian Ministries, Evangelism Resources, and the Overseas Council.

Only about 100 programs of higher education exist for evangelical leaders outside the West. Just two are more than 25 years old. In response, the Overseas Council has started the Institute for Excellence in Global Theological Education "to strengthen the leadership skills of presidents, principals, deans, and senior leaders of evangelical leadership programs" outside the West.[14]

Yet it is clear that other approaches need to be developed, too. Only about 5 percent of the 2 million pastors have formal training.[15] For years a prime ministry model has been to bring non-Western Christians to the West for theological training. But it has become clear that too many of these students, after a taste of freedom and prosperity, never return to their homelands where the need is greatest.

Even those who do return face problems. Ajith Fernando, national director of Youth for Christ in Sri Lanka, says some are no longer able to identify with the poor in their own country. "With their contacts abroad, these leaders can live on a higher level than their colleagues," Fernando noted. "They in turn help their colleagues, thus becoming their benefactors. This way they avoid a lot of the frustration that comes with identifying with the poor. Some send their children to national schools where the monthly fees are more than the monthly salary of an average Christian worker here. Many of them return to the West after a few years of service in Sri Lanka."[16]

Effective training of pastors in poorer parts of the world was a major theme at the Trainers of Pastors International Consultation (TOPIC) in Manila in 1999. Convened by RREACH International, following a preliminary conference at Wheaton College's Billy Graham Center in 1997, TOPIC's goal was to get agencies to work together to achieve the goal of having "every church with a trained pastor" and to launch a church health movement (not a church growth movement). TOPIC drew together the leaders of 96 organizations from 49 countries. All were involved in training pastors nonformally, that is, through study that does not lead to an academic degree.

"The task is bigger than any one group can possibly handle," stated RREACH's Ramesh Richard, chairman of the movement's steering committee. "Further, formal education simply cannot keep up with the explosive growth of the church worldwide. . . . It is our hope to minimize effort duplication, eliminate waste of resources, and thereby enhance missions impact. Indeed, an entirely new architecture for global missions is needed for the new millennium, beyond the traditional and indigenous missionary paradigms."[17]

Maturing missionaries

The non-Western missions movement is growing up in other ways, too. One is simply in the spreading desire to get the job of world evangelization done. It is no longer a novel idea for non-Westerners to assume responsibility for the Great Commission; both they and their Western partners (some of whom were their spiritual parents) now expect this. Indeed, some Westerners have been a little rankled by repeated statements that the center of gravity of missions has shifted from the North and West to the South and East. Now it is Westerners who are calling for partnership, as they see the churches they planted move ahead with the task. (See chapters 2, 11, and 16.)

Examples of the overseas church's budding missionary maturity are too numerous to mention. One will have to suffice.

In 1998 a team of ten Ethiopians from the SIM Kale Heywet churches and two American missionaries saw more than 1,300 people in Tamil Nadu in India make professions of faith in Christ during a three-month evangelistic ministry. The Ethiopians' familiarity with animism enabled them to connect with the Indians they ministered to. They also started choirs, youth and women's meetings, and organized discipleship programs in some of the churches. Howard Brant, SIM's strategic ministries director, commented, "Ethiopia has received the gospel for many years – and the time has come for this nation to start sending out missionaries into all the world."[18]

It's a call more and more non-Westerners, increasingly sure of themselves, are heeding.

FURTHER READING

"Stop sending money!" by Robertson McQuilkin, *Christianity Today,* 1 March 1999.

"The problem with success," by Chuck Bennett, *EMQ,* January 1996.

"A flaw in recruiting strategy?" by Joseph D'Souza, *EMQ,* April 2000.

"Some thoughts on missionary burnout," by Ajith Fernando, *EMQ,* October 1999.

DISCUSSION QUESTIONS

1. *What are some of the signs that the non-Western churches and missions agencies are coming of age? Have you seen any of them in your own ministry?*

2. *How should Western Christians interact with maturing non-Western Christians?*

3. *What programs does your church or agency have to encourage the maturation process?*

4. *What are some of the pitfalls of unwise assistance?*

Part IV
THE GLOBAL ARENA

Chapter 19

Global Culture

The British Foreign Office recently asked some of its embassies to comment on whether Islam or "the Coca-Cola culture is more attractive for the young generation of Arabs and Muslims." One diplomat told the *Washington Post*, "The last thing Syrians want to do is replace one restrictive dogmatic regime with another. They wear grunge. They want to make money." Another said, "The answer is that Islam is attractive and Coca-Cola is attractive, and there's enormous tension between the two of them."

Thailand's Buddhist priesthood is feeling the pressures of modernity, too. Fewer young men are entering monasteries, and those who do are taking lighter vows. "It is a dying tradition," one lecturer on Thai culture said. "We have had our own culture for thousands of years. But right now we are taking the culture of the Western countries, and in my opinion that is not good."

Increasing numbers of Asian governments believe that "growth produces legitimacy," according to Alex Magno, a political scientist at the University of the Philippines. "It is a thoroughly modern obsession with growth," Magno told the *New York Times*. "The fastest-growing sector is the middle class, and that middle class is not an Islamic or Buddhist or Catholic middle class. It is a middle class that is intoxicated with growth, whose own personal fortunes depend on the GNP rate."[1]

Here to stay

Representatives from 500 organizations – trade unionists, farmers, anarchists, and environmentalists – all found they had something in common at the 1999 World Trade Organization meetings in Seattle: their common hatred of globalization. In his book *The Lexus and the Olive Tree: Understanding Globalization*, journalist Thomas Friedman states, "The driving idea behind globalization is free-market capitalism – the more you let market forces rule and the more you open your economy to free trade and competition, the more efficient and flourishing your economy will be."[2]

Despite occasional hiccups, like the Asian and Russian financial crises, globalization seems here to stay. According to a recent United Nations survey, some 60,000 transnational business firms produce a fourth of the world's economic output. Capital flows by global investors have reached impressive, and sometimes destabilizing, levels. Far more private investment money goes into the poor world than does humanitarian assistance, a fact development professionals have come to recognize. Governments are being forced to revamp their economies not out of altruism toward their downtrodden citizens, but because outsiders demand it. Generally, the system rewards openness and transparency, both economic and political. "Globalization," Friedman writes, "is the overarching international system shaping the domestic politics and foreign relations of virtually every country."[3]

More than business

Of course, globalization involves more than business. It is also reflected in culture. Powered by the Internet revolution, the globe increasingly seems to be returning to a pre-Babel past. Old barriers are quickly falling to the consumer-driven revolution. The Berlin Wall and the Soviet empire it symbolized collapsed as citizens chained by communist ideology saw the higher living standards available in the West.

As the world becomes more interconnected, the global culture is bringing about other positive changes. "Despite the persistence of state-sponsored repression and genocidal conflict, the belief that individuals have a claim to basic rights and dignities is being embraced on every continent," the *New York Times* observed in 1999. "Freedom of speech and assembly, freedom from slavery, torture and arbitrary arrest, and the right to equality under the law as common values are still quite new in many parts of the world. But leaders who violate these principles now face international exposure, sanctions and even outside intervention, as Slobodan Milosevic discovered this year."[4]

Sometimes, however, the reality of the global culture seems a bit tarnished. A prominent slogan during the "velvet revolution" in the old Soviet client state of Czechoslovakia in 1989 was "Truth and love must prevail over lies and hatred." Later, one of the revolutionaries regretfully told the *Wall Street Journal* that freedom from communism has not been as idyllic as had been hoped. Materialism has won the day.

"People stopped smiling at each other and began thinking about themselves," he said. "There's a lack of love." Another stated, "We started out spiritual and ended up material."[5]

Electronic media, business opportunities, and popular culture are increasingly promoting the spread of a global culture founded upon the Enlightenment values of human reason and progress from its Western base to areas struggling to maintain their traditional identities. Mike Stachura has traveled to many of the world's ports with Operation Mobilization's ship ministry. "Thus far there has not been a culture that has been able to withstand the influences of modernization," he stated. "Whether it is a traditional agrarian society, an industrialized society, a closed, Marxist society, all – when given a major dose of modernization – are succumbing."[6]

The driving forces of modern culture – science and humanism – have put even Islam, the most insulated of all the major world religions, next in line for significant change. The Muslim religious book, the Qur'an, is quietly being subjected to some of the critical-historical analysis the Bible underwent in the 19th century.[7] Countries such as Kuwait, Algeria, Jordan, Yemen, and even Saudi Arabia are inching toward more democratic processes. Muslim liberals from Iran to Bangladesh are seeking to link democracy and political pluralism with Islamic principles.

Banks are offering mutual funds based on Islamic financial principles. But the going is seldom smooth. Chapter 20 describes the harsh reactions of radicals to these changes.

Modernity and missions

What of the non-Western churches and agencies, which constitute the world evangelical majority, and which now face modernity's inexorable advances over their airwaves, in their classrooms and ministries, and via their keyboards? Will the same Enlightenment that has so successfully attacked the biblical worldview that nurtured its birth now undermine the Asian, African, and Latin American churches just beginning to taste the fruits of scientific progress? While they will presumably have more resources to give to world missions as their economies continue to develop and their lifespans increase, the question is, will they still want to? H. Dan Beeby, a former missionary to Taiwan and China, wondered in the January 1994 issue of the *International Bulletin of Missionary Research*: "If the deep-down door of the European mind has been closed and shut out the Gospel, will the same happen in the rest of the world – in Korea, Taiwan, Kenya, Papua, and the uttermost parts of the world? Are we facing one world with one culture, and that culture Western secular culture? And will that culture be totally devoid of the categories that are integral to Christian belief?"[8]

Western culture has been blamed for everything from Soviet communism to Nazism to crumbling morality to environmental destruction, and credited with today's dramatically longer life expectancies, the Green Revolution, and spreading material prosperity. Which side is right? Both are. Missiologists are quick to acknowledge the advantages the modern world has bestowed – money, transportation, communication, instant access to information – and just as fast to express reservations.

Evangelicals have always been alert to embrace modern tools to spread the gospel, and rightly so. Percy Crawford aired the first evangelistic nationwide television program over half a century ago. The *Jesus* film has been seen by more than 2 billion people in more than 500 languages; its usefulness promises to be enhanced by its recent introduction in DVD format. SAT-7, a Christian satellite television service in the Middle East, is daily broadcasting the gospel to millions who have had little access to it. Far East Broadcasting Korea, meanwhile, has started a new station and a new transmitter that enable the agency to air 19 programs into the communist north, where free access to information is denied.[9]

"The ultimate fundamentalism"

Yet while technology enables Christians to transmit their message to wider audiences, it does not necessarily guarantee that the message will be understood, or that the messengers will remain the same. Saying that "evangelicals have been seduced by the spirit of the age," Bill Taylor, who heads the World Evangelical Fellowship's Missions Commission, charges that the American church has dichotomized life, made Christianity easy, wasted energy fighting itself, and accepted a low theology of culture: "Modernity and the postmodern value systems have sapped the very core and marrow of biblical Christianity."[10]

Beeby avers, "Modernity is the ultimate fundamentalism – dogmatic and exclusive. It cannot coexist. It is attractive and it is missionary. Professing tolerance it tolerates only itself. It is decimating European churches which have been so successful at mission overseas but are almost helpless in missionary endeavor at home."[11]

Culture currents in the church

Paul McKaughan, head of the Evangelical Fellowship of Mission Agencies, says evangelical influence on US culture is wide but not deep. "The church has almost become indistinguishable from the culture," McKaughan stated. "We talk about being salt and light in the culture, but usually we are talking about governmental institutions and culture in the abstract and not the personal or in collective demonstration. We are almost as materialistic. We are almost as fearful and reactionary as the society as a whole."[12] (For more on this theme, see chapters 3 and 5.) Other critics wonder about the ways technology shapes our thinking and creates gaps between the rich and poor worlds.

Critics like Samuel Escobar, an evangelical theologian and missiologist from Peru, and Jim Engel, an evangelical marketing specialist, fault the US missions movement for succumbing to "managerial missiology," the belief that missions can be approached like a business problem. With the right inputs, the thinking goes, the right outcomes can be assured. Any number of approaches have been hailed as the "key" to world evangelization or to reaching particular groups – everything from contextualization to saturation evangelization. Most, while successful up to a point, also have been shown to have limits.

McKaughan says that mission organizations have reflected their secular counterparts for the last 40 or 50 years, particularly in the areas of the professionalization and institutionalization of missions. "This mirror-like image is far too close for comfort," he said. "We have come through an extended time of institutionalization. We felt that we could organize and manage our way to world evangelization. The natural laws that seem to control the rest of institutional life seem to shape us, as well."[13]

Stachura says that Christians in the non-Western world, unlike their Western counterparts, have seen the wave of modernization coming and so are able to surf it rather than be drowned by it. "They are very aware of the effects of modernization," he says. "It's not like it's creeping up on them. I think it crept up on us, and we bought in. . . . It's coming much faster and much harder to them."

Non-Western Christian are staying afloat by using coping strategies such as emphasizing biblical truth in their proclamation, rejecting materialism, and developing small groups – strategies which focus on the unfulfilled promises of the modern world, exemplified by a growing gap between modern society's haves and have-nots. Stachura points out, "They're not coming and offering that your life is going to get better in terms of stuff."[14]

Postmodernism's perils

Modernity is not the only element of threat in today's global culture. "The West is becoming Easternized and the East is becoming Westernized," Dallas Theological Seminary's Michael Pocock said, pointing to a worldwide homogenizing effect. "In terms of being satisfying, materialism has been found wanting."[15]

Postmodernism, disillusionment with materialism and a rejection of the knowability of truth, may present more insidious challenges to Great Commission Christians. At a 1999 evangelical missions theology conference in Brazil, attended by evangelical missionaries from around the world, some of the younger participants expressed discomfort with claims of "absolute truth," which they linked with a history of oppression.[16]

While it is true that there have been some sorry episodes in church history associated with claims to enforce absolute truth – most notably, perhaps, the Crusades and the Inquisition – any claim that these events were wrong is based itself on absolute truth. Christianity without truth is mere wishful thinking. Without it, we must part ways not only with the things we don't like about religion, but also those we do. The question for the evangelical in this postmodern age should not be whether there is absolute truth, but where it can be found. Jesus' claims to absolute truth are the bones and ligaments holding Christianity together. "I am the way and the truth and the life," Jesus said. "No one comes to the Father except through me."

Another danger, Robertson McQuilkin warns, is cultural relativism. "This has been the premise of cultural anthropology and, though these presuppositions do not control missiological thinking in evangelical circles, they have seeped into our thinking sufficiently to distort biblical thinking on key missions issues."[17]

Pocock says today's missionary movement is potentially more syncretistic in its willingness to borrow from the insights of anthropology and cultural anthropology. "Those sciences teach us to value other cultures," Pocock observed. "You're seeing that in the spiritual mapping and territorial spirits area, where I believe we are saying to a much greater degree, 'Animistic cultures have perceived spiritual realities correctly, and there's something to learn from them.'"[18]

Pocock notes that postmodern pessimism about what people can accomplish through their own creativity and ingenuity also threatens missions outreach, particularly in places like Korea and Singapore, where missionary efforts are now vigorous. "When a group gets gripped by pessimism, this can also affect the church," Pocock says. "[People] stop thinking that they've got solutions for the rest of the world that ought to be exported, like the missionary movement."[19]

An opportunity

If evangelicals can hold onto the gospel amid these cultural currents, postmodernism presents an opportunity. Stachura says that the very name "postmodern" means that the emerging era is a transition into something not yet known. He says people in the postmodern world recognize a void in their souls and are looking for spiritual reality, truth, and relationship, all of which Christ provides. "They are looking for something that is real," Stachura said. "I find that to be incredibly good. It breaks through pretense, it breaks through programs, it breaks through and cuts down to the kind of stuff that Jesus was about."[20]

Taylor says churches and agencies need to adapt to the postmoderns in their midst to harness them for ministry in an increasingly postmodern world. "Churches and Christian leadership committed to world missions will have to be much more creative than they are now to generate enthusiasm and mechanisms for the Generation X role in world evangelism," he said. "Their young, creative leadership will probably be released to create new ways of doing missions. More power to them. I have three Generation X kids, and they have taught me volumes about radical discipleship and outreach to their generation. Now to turn this to global missions!"[21]

But to take advantage of the opportunity, Stachura and others say, the church needs to be reawakened. "Right now the American church, particularly in its relationship to missions, has been struggling for the last 20 years to try and be the majority church," he said. "You go back to the Book of Acts and you realize the church was never the majority church. It was always a committed group in the minority. They were up against incredible odds. They never thought they would win the whole culture to their side."

"The really growing churches in the missions-focused Two-Thirds World have an awful lot to say about being a persecuted minority, being a church that realizes that we aren't going to have tremendous resources, but we don't care because we have Christ."[22]

McKaughan says the pendulum may indeed be swinging back to persecution. "Christ's church will remain," McKaughan said. "We, however, may occupy the more historically characteristic station of a persecuted minority at odds with the values of the larger society than an honored or recognized participant and supporter of that society."[23]

FURTHER READING

Discipling Nations: The Power of Truth to Transform Cultures, by Darrow Miller, with Stan Guthrie (Seattle: YWAM, 1998).

Faith and Modernity, edited by Philip Sampson, Vinay Samuel, and Chris Sugden (Oxford: Lynx Communications, 1994).

"The pitfalls and perils of electronic communications," by Rick Cruse, *EMQ*, July 1996.

The Lexus and the Olive Tree: Understanding Globalization, by Thomas Friedman (New York: Farrar, Straus & Giroux, 1999).

Faster: The Acceleration of Just About Everything, by James Gleick (New York: Pantheon Books, 1999).

Mustard Seed versus McWorld, by Tom Sine (Grand Rapids: Baker, 1999).

Scripture and Strategy, by David J. Hesselgrave (Pasadena: William Carey Library, 1994).

No Place for Truth, by David Wells (Grand Rapids: Eerdmans, 1993).

God in the Wasteland, by David Wells (Grand Rapids: Eerdmans/ Leicester: InterVarsity Press, 1994).

Dining with the Devil, by Os Guinness (Grand Rapids: Baker, 1993).

DISCUSSION QUESTIONS

1. *Define globalization, modernism, and postmodernism. How have you seen them at work?*

2. *How do you feel about the Bible's claims to absolute truth?*

3. *In what ways might globalization affect churches in the non-Western world?*

4. *How should the evangelical church respond if it becomes increasingly marginalized?*

Chapter 20

Radical Reactions

Fifty-eight-year-old Graham Staines never received the accolades of a Mother Teresa. A native of Australia, Staines had spent half his life quietly ministering to India's forgotten poor. A missionary with the Brisbane-based Evangelical Missionary Society, Staines directed clinics for lepers in the eastern state of Orissa. In the remote village of Manoharpur, he was respected by Christian and Hindu alike.

On 22 January 1999, Staines and his two sons, Philip, 10, and Timothy, 6, attended the annual meeting of the church there. After it was over, the three climbed into their automobile to get some sleep before attempting the five-hour drive back to their home in Baripada the next morning. At about 1 a.m., a mob of as many as 100 young men arrived, chanting to the Hindu monkey god, "Long live Hanuman!" As sleepy villagers stumbled out of their homes to see what was happening, the men set fire to the vehicle. Graham, Philip, and Timothy never had a chance.[1]

Angry backlash

Today, at the launch of the third millennium, the spread of capitalism around the globe has opened peoples from Iran to China to new opportunities, new technologies, and new ways of thinking. However, it has also sparked an angry backlash in some quarters against anything associated with modernity. For better or worse, Christianity is often equated with the modern world and thus is blamed for its ills, everything from the breakdown of the family to the expansion of social pathologies such as pornography and gambling. Christians can only applaud those who stand against these evils and join with them in fighting the darkest expressions of mankind's sinful nature. There are many nonviolent Hindus, Muslims, and Buddhists who stand ready to work with us in the cause of decency. The question is, are we ready and willing to build bridges to them wherever possible?

Yet for a pluralistic age that sometimes seems to place tolerance at the pinnacle of the virtues, ours is an increasingly intolerant world. Abdelfattah Amor, the United Nations special rapporteur on religious intolerance, says extremism is on the rise throughout the world. "No religion is free from extremism," he said in a report. Noting the persistence of Islamic extremism in Afghanistan, Bangladesh, Indonesia, Niger, and Pakistan, Abdelfattah noted, "It is evident that this phenomenon has spread to other religions, as seen by the rise of Hindu extremism directed against Christian and Muslim communities and, potentially, against religious minorities in India, and even in Nepal."[2]

In 1996 Samuel Huntington wrote a controversial book, *The Clash of Civilizations and the Remaking of World Order*,[3] asserting that the post-Cold War world is being divided along religious and cultural fault lines, and that there is little that can be done to stop the process. While his thesis was unpopular among the crowd seeking the spread of business and democracy (not necessarily in that order), time has proven it surprisingly accurate.

Indian thinker Vishal Mangalwadi, author of *India: The Grand Experiment*, writes, "The collapse of secular ideologies – communism, socialism, liberalism – has created an ideological vacuum in Asia that is being filled rapidly by Hindu, Muslim, and Buddhist worldviews."[4]

Islamists control the rules of debate in Indonesia and the Arab world; radical Buddhists are cracking down on Christians in Sri Lanka; and right-wing Hindus are terrorizing Christians in India. Muslim revolutionaries in Central Asia kidnapped a

Western missionary, Herb Gregg, and released him months later – with part of his index finger severed. Even in the United States of Amalgamation, extremism is appearing in various guises. Abortion clinic bombers, white supremacist hate groups, largely lawless militias, church arsonists, and student gunmen have rejected the polite rules of civil discourse. Instead, they have bought into Mao's dictum that power comes from the barrel of a gun.

Longtime missionary captives Tim Van Dyke, 43, and Steve Welsh, also 43, were killed on 19 June 1995, during a clash between their guerrilla captors and a Colombian military patrol. The pair had been missing since 16 January 1994, when they were abducted from the New Tribes Mission base at Villavicencio. Three others with New Tribes – David Mankins, Mark Rich, and Richard Tenenoff – have been missing since 31 January 1993, when they were kidnapped by Colombian rebels in Púcuro, Panama.

Christians who take the Great Commission seriously rightly wonder what this reactionary trend means for missions. But hostility, while daunting, need not be the end of the story. In the face of such unrelenting resistance to the gospel, missiologists are looking for fresh answers. Some are coming to acknowledge the spiritual dimensions of the problem. While contextualization – the attempt to accurately communicate the transcultural gospel in culturally palatable ways – continues to play a dominant role in current missions thinking (see chapter 12), many strategists and lay people are seeking spiritual keys through the biblically dubious approach of confronting demonic "territorial spirits" through spiritual mapping, prayer walks, and other methods (see chapter 9). Other Christian strategists, with more scriptural warrant, report breakthroughs in "power encounters" between Christ and the agents of darkness, particularly in the non-Western world.

Still, missionaries, overseas Christians, and evangelical scholars are employing a variety of innovative cross-cultural strategies, supported by prayer, to reach the unreached and resistant peoples of the world. Increasing numbers of agencies are "recruiting for the frontiers," directing recruits to previously neglected areas such as the so-called 10/40 Window (see chapter 7).

Yet the going is slow. Nik Repkin notes that among Muslims living in the Horn of Africa, only one person per church-based evangelical agency per year is becoming a believer in Christ. Meanwhile, 80 percent of Muslim "seekers" in the Horn of Africa have returned to Islam.[5] Yet in one sense Islam, Hinduism, and Buddhism have always been rocky paths to sowers of the gospel. Another age-old truth is that comparatively few missionaries have even attempted to share the good news with these people, which some strategists have called the "crisis of missions."[6] Dudley Woodberry estimates that only 2 percent of the world missionary force is working among Muslims.[7] The distribution of missionaries among the world's other major religions is even less.

What follows is a survey of key areas, religions, and peoples experiencing religious reaction, along with a brief look at missionary efforts to reach them with the gospel.

The Hindus

The world's estimated 719 million Hindus have long been objects of missionary concern. William Carey, the so-called "father of modern missions," began his ministry among the Hindus of India two centuries ago. Today, the Christian presence in India could be characterized as a mile wide and an inch deep. While every one of the country's 600 districts has a Christian presence, only about a fourth of its 28,000 postal regions have a Protestant pastor, church, or missionary. Only a third of India's 219 languages possess any portion of Christian Scripture.[8] Only 1 percent of the country, despite nearly 2 millennia of Christian presence, would call itself evangelical. Much evangelistic work in India focuses on the relatively responsive tribal peoples and on the poor (who are often one and the same). This activity is now sparking a backlash in places like Orissa.

India, the world's largest democracy, is currently run by the rightist Bharatiya Janata Party. The BJP is widely believed to have been behind the 1992 destruction of a 16th-century mosque in Ayodhya that sparked rioting that left nearly a thousand Muslims dead. Moving away from the constitutionally enshrined right to freedom of religion, the BJP prime minister has called for a national debate on conversion. Efforts are under way to legally restrict matters of conscience. One bill, ostensibly designed to protect freedom of religion, would do just the opposite, according to Joseph D'Souza, chairman and CEO of the All India Christian Council. This group was formed in response to attacks, both verbal and physical, in recent years. "The bill is neither designed for freedom, nor for the growth and maturing of religion," he said. "All religions are missionary religions, including Hinduism. The bill makes a mockery of India being a signatory of the UN Convention on Human Rights."[9]

The tactics of others in the nationalist movement are more direct. In 1998 and 1999, more than 100 religiously motivated attacks on Christians were documented, including the murder of the Staines. Many were directed against Catholics – nuns were raped, churches were destroyed.

Pope John Paul II's visit to India in November 1999 highlighted some of the tensions. Some Hindu militants burned him in effigy in many places before he arrived in New Delhi. Others warned they would not allow him to set foot on Indian soil. Even some 300 Asian bishops, cowed or co-opted by the radical Hindus, publicly opposed any renewed efforts at evangelization. The pope, to his great credit, not only came anyway, but also presented a strong and yet sensitive rationale for Catholics to, in the words of Mangalwadi, "remake their continent Christianity's home during the next millennium."[10]

Hostility to Christians in India was also stimulated by the publication of a pocket guide intended to help Southern Baptists pray for Hindus, portrayed as lost, during the Divali festival of lights in 1999. Responding to this hostility, the International Mission Board stated: "The language in the prayer guide was chosen to communicate to Southern Baptists, not Hindus, and the truths in it, as we understand them, are rooted in the Bible, the book we believe to be God's revealed word. It is distressing to us that elements of the guide may have offended our Hindu neighbors and for that we are profoundly sorry."[11]

Yet some Hindus have been receptive to the gospel. In largely tribal north-east India, churches continue to grow rapidly. Nepal, the world's only Hindu kingdom, has seen explosive church multiplication. The evangelical presence in this poor nation has grown from 25 baptized believers in 1960 to more than 300,000 today.[12] Literature distribution, film teams, miraculous "power encounters," and healing ministries have all played a part. However, some of India's radical groups are reported to be setting up shop there, with the goal of halting the conversions.

In contrast, few upper-caste Hindus in India's north have been confronted with the claims of Christ. According to Robin Thomson of South Asian Concern, a ministry based in Britain, many Hindus see the church as a Western institution fit only for the marginalized members of society. Their pride in Hindu culture presents a major obstacle. "For the minority who get past the cultural barrier, a major spiritual barrier is the gospel's emphasis on the cross, repentance, and salvation by grace alone," he says. "Many Hindus have a deep desire to do things for their salvation and a deep pride in their culture and spiritual achievement."[13]

Christians, and not always traditional missionaries, are tackling these strongholds head on. Mangalwadi has dealt with Hindu cultural misperceptions in books such as *The Great Missionary Conspiracy* and *Truth and Social Reform*. Meanwhile, a Christian scholarly journal published in Madras called *Dharma Deepika* is directed to Hindu, Buddhist, and Christian religious leaders. Christian businessmen are being encouraged to go to India, which is attempting to implement market reforms, and influence the highest echelons for Christ. A coalition of ministries called Partnership for North India has, for its part, set ambitious evangelization and church-planting goals.

It is a start, but only that. Thomson states, "We are just beginning the task of serious communication of the good news of Jesus Christ with Hindus. There is a great foundation of the demonstration of Christ's love and justice through Christian service over the last 200 years. We now need to share the good news in ways that are sensitive to culture."[14]

The Muslims

Sensitivity to culture is a continuing concern of many who are trying to reach the world's 1 billion Muslims for Christ. Many Muslims were infuriated when Western investigators almost immediately identified pilot suicide as the cause of the 1999 crash of an EgyptAir jet, which killed 217 people. They were offended because what was offered as evidence for this theory was the cockpit voice recorder, which picked up a pilot saying a short prayer shortly before the plane went into its fatal dive. "Perhaps more than anything, this claim will contribute to extremism and anti-Americanism in the region," a professor on the West Bank told the *Wall Street Journal*. "It's an insult to the integrity of Islam and any human being. I'm not religious, but I'm insulted."[15]

Just as there is no typical Christian, Muslims come in many varieties. Missionary Joshua Massey notes three main types: those (such as some Iranians) who are disillusioned with Islam; others (perhaps Central Asians or those in the Balkans) who are ambivalent about their religion; and a large bloc (from the Arab world, Indonesia, and South Asia) who are content with their beliefs. Each group has myriad gradations.[16]

In 1998 FEBA Radio, in consultation with local Christians and expatriates in the South Asian island nation of Maldives, began broadcasting Christian programming in Dhivehi, the local language. The response was immediate: the Islamic government, which prided itself on the republic's 100 percent Muslim status, kicked out all foreign Christians "for life" and rounded up and jailed Maldivians suspected of being Christians. The locals were eventually released, but a message had been sent. A missionary observer noted, "The local media called the radio program the greatest attack on their nation since the Portuguese conquest in the 16th century."[17]

Of course, many Muslims now live in the West. Jay Smith, an American Brethren in Christ missionary, has drawn fire for his willingness to publicly debate Muslims in Europe. Some Christians see his approach as insensitive and overly confrontational. Smith, however, and his growing numbers of admirers see the ministry as necessary to advance truth among Muslims. "We think we are being Christlike by conceding many salient points when 'dialoguing' with them," he told journalist Deann Alford in *World Pulse*. "But in reality, the message that they are hearing is that we aren't sure where we stand."[18]

Now more than two decades after Iran's Islamic Revolution, many people there, particularly young people, aren't sure where they stand. Not liking what they have seen of Islam, they are looking elsewhere for meaning in life. Rebelling against the strict religion imposed by the late Ayatollah Khomeini, who once said, "There is no fun in Islam," they are desperately searching for fun, and for a loosening of religious restrictions. At the risk of violence at the hands of the brutal religious police, they are experimenting with romance, drinking, drugs, parties, the Internet, and even political freedom. Students were instrumental in the overthrow of the shah, and these young people, disillusioned with Islam, may yet be instrumental in ushering in a revolution of a different sort. They were the force that elected a Muslim moderate, Mohammad Khatami, as Iran's president, and some of them have clashed already with the mullahs.

The Buddhists

The Buddhist world, with over half a billion people, has long been resistant to Christianity. South Korea is the only largely Buddhist nation that has had a significant turning to Christ. Despite a large missionary presence in Japan, few citizens there have embraced Christ.

For the last half century, the Buddhist majority of Sri Lanka has been pursuing a political agenda attempting to institute a Buddhist state. That state, however, has little room for Hindus and Christians. In the 1960s, Christians became associated with the country's colonial past and were charged with "immorality, drunkenness, and alien vices." Yet a largely lay Christian movement has taken the gospel to virtually every village, starting in the 1980s. Buddhist radicals are responding with arson, assault, and legal harassment.[19]

One reason for the lack of evangelistic fruit among Buddhists worldwide, of course, is that Buddhism has received comparatively little evangelistic attention from Western Christians. That is beginning to change, not because more are going to Buddhist heartlands like Sri Lanka and Myanmar, but because the Buddhists are coming to them. Thanks to increased immigration and slick public relations, this religion of renunciation has successfully transplanted itself on consumerist American soil. Fueled by glowing movie portrayals, interest in the Dalai Lama and Tibet, and celebrity endorsements from Phil Jackson, Richard Gere, and other Buddhists, the religion (along with Hinduism and Islam) is busily propagating in North America.

"Their influence is very powerful," stated former Soka Gakkai (Japan-based) Buddhist James Stephens, founder of the Sonrise Center for Buddhist Studies, one of the few evangelical agencies specifically focusing on the religion. "Buddhists look at America as a mission field, as a prime mission field."[20]

The Jews

Another resistant religion with influence far beyond its numbers is Judaism, which has 14 million adherents worldwide. A June 1996 resolution of the Southern Baptist Convention reaffirming the validity of evangelizing Jews provoked a predictable firestorm of criticism from many Jewish leaders – and forced evangelical groups to ponder their missiological priorities.

Judaism, like Islam, has a wide spectrum of followers, from the highly secular to the ultra-orthodox. In recent years Israel has received many Russian Jews whose commitment to Judaism is, at best, weak. Authorities have questioned whether, in fact, they are really Jews. Significant numbers of these newcomers have responded positively to the gospel of their Messiah, Jesus. The authorities, used to a religious monopoly in the Jewish state, have responded by attempting to criminalize evangelism and literature distribution, though their efforts have been largely rebuffed. The latest attempt would slap a five-year prison sentence on anyone convicted of soliciting or persuading anyone to change religion. In some circumstances, the penalty could double. Jewish radicals even seek to impose their will on Jews who are not, in their opinion, Jewish enough. One member of the Israeli parliament, the Knesset, prompted an outcry by saying that Israel is a democratic and multicultural state. The radicals say that it is a Jewish state – and that they will define who is a Jew.[21]

In recent decades, groups such as Jews for Jesus have provided the intellectual justification for "messianic" congregations, which retain and celebrate the Jewish roots of the Christian faith. Growing numbers of such churches have sprung up among the world's 60,000 or so believing Jews. "Wherever you go among Jews," states Fuller Seminary missiologist Arthur Glasser, "you find now that there are messianic congregations of believing Jews – not just Jews who have melted into the wallpaper of Gentile Christianity."[22]

The role of sacrifice

Even among groups that are indifferent or hostile to Christ, self-sacrificing commitment to him is noticed. Graham Staines's ministry among the poor and his senseless death have prompted much soul-searching in India. "The people loved him," stated Joseph D'Souza, director of Operation Mobilization India in Secunderabad. "Who on earth would leave the comfort of Australia, live, and labor in such conditions? No wonder the president of India lamented that we had killed a man we should have modeled."[23]

FURTHER READING

"The Context of Kinship: Jihad and McWorld," by Doug McConnell, AERDO Occasional Paper No. 7 <www.aerdo. org/occasion7.htm>.

The Clash of Civilizations and the Remaking of World Order, by Samuel P. Huntington (New York: Simon & Schuster, 1996).

Reaching the Resistant: Barriers and Bridges for Mission, edited by Dudley Woodberry (Pasadena: William Carey Library, 1998).

Faiths in Conflict? Christian Integrity in a Multicultural World, by Vinoth Ramachandra (Leicester: InterVarsity Press, 1999).

DISCUSSION QUESTIONS

1. *What are some of the factors causing a religious backlash among religious people worldwide?*

2. *How do you feel about working with members of other religions to stand against evils of the modern world? When should we not work with them?*

3. *How should our mission approach differ with people who are dissatisfied with the religion in which they were raised?*

4. *How do you feel about suffering and sacrifice if these are needed to reach reactionaries with the gospel?*

5. *In what ways is evangelicalism a reactive movement in the USA?*

Chapter 21

Persecution and Religious Liberty

Following the unexpected ascension of Olusegun Obasanjo, an evangelical Christian and a reformer, to Nigeria's presidency in May 1999, Christians quietly rejoiced, hoping for a fresh start for their poor and corruption-ridden nation. Muslims, however, began agitating for the adoption of Islamic sharia law across the mostly Muslim northern states. In Kaduna, on 21 February 2000, Muslim youths attacked a peaceful protest of thousands of Christians, killing a student from the Baptist seminary. The next morning, a mob attacked the campus, killing 11 more. They set all the buildings on fire, causing an estimated $5.3 million in damage. Overall, more than 1,000 people have died in Muslim-Christian violence across northern Nigeria since the push for Muslim law began.[1]

A growing movement

At the beginning of the 1990s, a handful of evangelical Christian agencies tried in vain to generate concern for their persecuted brethren around the world, either in Washington, DC, or among fellow Christians. That has changed decisively. The International Day of Prayer for the Persecuted Church (IDOP) has both powered much of this newfound interest and ridden its crest. The 1999 day of prayer linked perhaps 120 million Christians from an estimated 300,000 churches and agencies in 130 nations in prayer for the persecuted. IDOP is sponsored by the World Evangelical Fellowship, in partnership with agencies such as

Open Doors with Brother Andrew, Voice of the Martyrs, Christian Solidarity Worldwide, and others.

"The International Day of Prayer is a day during which the body of Christ unites to remember, to pray, and to commit ourselves to be a voice for the voiceless," said Johan Candelin, director and coordinator for the annual event, which began in 1996. "Now, more than ever, we need to stand together in prayer for our brothers and sisters who are suffering for a faith all of us share."[2]

While the "now, more than ever," part of the statement may be grist for a good argument, no one disputes the need for prayer. As economic and political freedoms continue their slow, sometimes haphazard, diffusion around the world, religious liberty has often been a neglected stepchild. Until evangelicals, powerfully assisted by Michael Horowitz, a DC-based freedom advocate, who is himself Jewish, made it an issue, few secular agencies even noticed the barbarous treatment believers face around the world.

Playing politics

While IDOP is strictly nonpolitical in its orientation and practice, not everything done for persecuted Christians meets that standard. That's not necessarily all bad, but there are sometimes unintended costs. After several years of intense lobbying, religious rights advocates were pleased when the Clinton Administration signed into law the International Religious Freedom Act of 1998. The law requires the State Department to issue an annual report spotlighting abuses. Governments with the most systematic and egregious violations run the risk of incurring economic sanctions. The first report, in 1999, sparked protests from Beijing and Delhi, which denied the substance of the charges and complained of interference in their internal affairs.

What might be the long-term effects of punitive government enforcement of religious freedom? Some historians say that the Christian church went downhill spiritually after Constantine's

Edict of Milan in 313. In effect, the church has done better as a persecuted minority than it has as part of the establishment. Leery of any government coercion in religious matters, even when done for a good cause, some evangelicals question the sanctions approach. Missionaries are still trying to live down the charge of imperialism, which has stuck to them like mud for the last 100 years. Do we really want to depend on the power of the state again? Some Christians in China, for instance, complained that they, who were most affected, were hardly consulted before the law was passed.

An example that illustrates the dangers of a political approach involves several missionaries and an Egyptian who were arrested in Cairo a few years ago, before the act was even being considered. The authorities, angered that the group had upset religious sensibilities during an Islamic festival, threw them in prison. That might have been the last anyone heard of the group, except for the fact that the missionaries were Americans. Before leaving for Cairo, they had informed several US congressmen what they were planning to do and that they might require some assistance.

When the Egyptian government turned down a formal US government request to release the missionaries as a humanitarian act, one of the congressmen, who was on a committee in charge of foreign aid, threatened Egypt with the loss of all foreign aid. Egypt, which is the United States' largest recipient, was forced to capitulate. The Americans were released, and then expelled from the country. Their Egyptian co-worker, however, was transferred to a mental hospital where he underwent psychological torture.

Writing about the incident, Ralph Covell, a former missionary to China, said, "We may save our necks by an appeal to our government. But what are the consequences for God's kingdom?"[3]

Still, there is evidence that evangelical political involvement has ameliorated some abuses. In 1999 Uzbekistan authorities were holding five Christians. Observers from Compass Direct, a religious liberty news service, said they were religious prisoners. They were later released, just weeks before the State Department issued its annual report. "When they were sentenced," a source told Compass Direct, "it was reported on television and in the press. But they were freed very quietly."[4]

"That's the great blessing of having a strong country behind you," Pedro Moreno of Prison Fellowship said. "It's God's providence that the USA is powerful. . . . There is some negative influence, but the positive influence is amazing. Who would care about confronting Kuwait . . . if not the US? Who would confront China if not the US?"[5]

Meanwhile, the International Justice Mission, founded by Gary Haugen, an evangelical human rights lawyer, has brought about the release of more than 700 people suffering various forms of abuse – sometimes at government hands.[6] The World Evangelical Fellowship's Religious Liberty Commission (RLC) has been given observer status with the United Nations Human Rights Commission, raising the profile of the persecuted to unprecedented levels in the world body. The RLC organized prayer for 13 foreign Christians who were jailed in Saudi Arabia in October 1999. Weeks later, all were deported, unharmed. Such is not always the case among non-Western expatriates.[7] Clearly, vigilance is needed.

Persecution: the numbers

Open Doors maintains a list of the countries where religious persecution occurs. Nine of the ten worst offending countries on a recent list were Islamic states.[8] The only other country in the top ten was communist China, which persecutes not only Christians but Tibetan Buddhists, Muslims, and even the Falun Gong sect – any group the insecure leaders deem a threat.

The examples of China and North Korea (which is also high on the Open Doors list) show that Christianity in Asia is no stranger to persecution, thanks to strengthening nationalism and totalitarianism. Likewise in Eastern and Central Europe and Latin America, a minority but growing evangelical presence often faces opposition from established churches looking to maintain their position – and willing to stir up nationalistic passions and the power of the state to get their way, if need be.

In anarchic places in Africa, it can be hard for outsiders to distinguish to what degree violence is religiously motivated. For example, in Rwanda's 1994 ethnic genocide, many people were slaughtered inside churches. In fact, many clergy were specifically targeted for death. Even in the West, where the concept of religious liberty first took root, some of its fruit is beginning to wither. Christian groups like the Salvation Army have been labeled cults in highly secular places like France.

John Hanford, an aide to former US Senator Richard Lugar, has stated, "On a worldwide basis, Christians are the most persecuted major religion in terms of direct punishment for practicing religious activities – public worship, evangelism, charity."[9]

Around the world, Open Doors has counted some 500 Christians in prison because of their faith. Two hundred of them are imprisoned in Peru, where Christians are often wrongfully accused of aiding terrorists. Other countries where Christians are imprisoned include China (166 prisoners), Vietnam (52 prisoners), Iran and Saudi Arabia (13 prisoners each), Sudan (11), Egypt (8), Turkey and Colombia (4 each). Open Doors calls its accounting the "tip of the iceberg."[10]

Yet the extent of the problem is not really known. Some of the figures and anecdotes that make their way back to Christians in the West, however, are clearly inflated. Respected missions statisticians David Barrett and Todd Johnson, for instance, claim there are about 165,000 Christian martyrs annually around the world,[11] and their numbers, as many statistics are, have been picked up and repeated in the Christian media. But where all these martyrs come from is a mystery. Christians are undoubtedly dying for their faith. But the death of a Graham Staines in India (see chapter 20) or the occasional execution of a handful of evangelical pastors in Iran usually makes for big news in the evangelical media. Where is the evidence for tens of thousands of martyrs? While the international media have long ignored the issue, it does not seem credible that killing on such a massive scale could long remain undetected in today's media marketplace, where the exhuming of even several hundred bodies in Kosovo makes the ten o'clock news. To put it crudely, where are the bodies?

In India, during a recent 13-month span, some 140 acts of anti-Christian violence were counted across the sprawling country of a billion people. These acts were catalogued and protested vociferously. But as bad as they were, there were not thousands of deaths, which would be expected in a country that size – if the 165,000 martyrs estimate were true.

During 1999, Christian activists reported on the Internet that Christians were being killed in China, about the time Beijing was cracking down on the Falun Gong sect. An evangelical China expert tried in vain to confirm the reports.

Where, then, are the 165,000? Sudan arguably has the worst ongoing persecution. Since 1983 the Muslim and Arab north has been attempting to impose Islamic law on the Christian and animist south. Many black African Christians from the rebellious south have been raped and enslaved by northern Arabs. Some 1.9 million people have died since 1983 in the civil war. There have even been reports of Christians being crucified for their beliefs. But are they all martyrs? Not likely, since martyrs do not carry guns or commit their own atrocities, as southern rebels do. War is not martyrdom.

Yes, Christians are being slaughtered by the hundreds in religiously motivated mayhem in both Nigeria and Indonesia. Yet again, the violence is often two-way, and the numbers still do not justify the inflated estimate of 165,000 martyrs.

In fact, Christians are being persecuted from Burma to Maldives. But there are nowhere near the numbers of martyrs sometimes claimed. Such overhyped figures cheapen the sacrifice the real martyrs are called to make and bring their cause into disrepute.

Church attitudes

Whatever the true figures, religious liberty cases are assuming a new prominence, and rightly so. Brian O'Connell, a former director of the Religious Liberty Commission, says that for the first time non-Western Christians, seeing the role believers played in the collapse of Soviet communism, are willing to speak out and let their brothers and sisters in the West know about their plight. "Heretofore there has been a reluctance to publicly talk about the problems that they are facing," he said.[12] And O'Connell praises a new spirit of cooperation among Christian ministries focused on persecution.

However, another problem, according to Moreno, may be the church itself. "The church in many places is bringing the persecution upon itself," said Moreno, a native of Bolivia. "It's seen as an irrelevant group of fanatics jumping up and down, clapping and singing, but not really concerned about society, not really looking to the future."[13]

Power of prayer

O'Connell, for his part, says the battle against persecution is waged in three arenas – politics, public awareness, and prayer – but that many evangelicals tend to confine themselves to the first, urging that money be raised, laws passed, and foreign ministers harangued. He says the most important thing Christians can do is pray. "I don't want to underestimate, as sometimes we have done even in the evangelical community, the power of prayer," O'Connell said. "When we talk to people on the front lines in Egypt and Pakistan and say, 'Look, there are thousands of churches, there are millions of believers praying for you on a regular basis,' most people can't understand the impact that has on their lives, the peace that brings, the confidence that stirs."[14]

And yet, as bad as persecution is, God has used it ever since New Testament days to expand and strengthen the church. Agreeing with Romanian churchman Josef Tson that persecution is a "weapon of the church," O'Connell says that sometimes it is simply a sign that the church is doing its job. "My argument is that the reason we are being persecuted is because we are winning, not because we're losing. . . . The threat that the Islamic world feels from the Christian community is a very real one, because they realize that it challenges, at the very core, their understanding of what life is."[15]

Growth amid persecution

While this is by no means universal, there are encouraging signs of church growth in some situations of persecution, particularly in the Muslim world. Take the case of Sudan, a country where 70 percent of the country's 28 million people are said to be Muslims. The civil war instigated by the Arab military regime in Khartoum to force Islamic law on Sudan's Christian and animist people in the south has left between 3 million and 5 million homeless. Still, the news is not all bleak. Persistent reports indicate a surprising degree of religious freedom in the north, where many southerners have fled for protection. The *Jesus* film is shown freely there to refugees.

Revival is said to be spreading in the south, as well. The bishop of the Episcopal Church of Sudan, Nathaniel Garang, estimates that before the conflagration began 15 percent of the people of the south were Christians. Today, three-fourths may be.[16]

Clive Calver, president of the church-based international agency World Relief, guesses that there are a million more evangelical believers in the south than there were in 1982. An Episcopal bishop told him, "I had 12 churches. Now I have a thousand church groups."[17]

Or take the case of Iran. In 1994 three prominent Christian leaders were murdered in Iran, and church services in Farsi, the main language, were forbidden. Muslim converts and other Protestants continue to face arrest, imprisonment, and torture, despite the more liberal government. Iran's underground church has an estimated 15,000 or more members – half of them Muslim converts, according to Iranian Christians International.[18] Sources in the country say that perhaps tens of thousands or even more have converted to Christianity as disappointment with the Islamic leaders in Tehran spreads.

In Egypt, Christians have been murdered by Muslim extremists for years and the government continues to place unfair legal restrictions on churches, yet the church grows. An evangelical Coptic priest named Father Sama'an has a church of thousands who meet in a cave. Cairo's Kasr el-Dobara Evangelical Church, meanwhile, has a weekly attendance of 4,000. It recently hosted an outreach by international evangelist Luis Palau. The Bible Society of Egypt has reported a dramatic upswing in interest in the Christian Scriptures in recent years.[19]

Across North Africa, in fact, the church, basically stamped out for over a millennium, is being resurrected. Arab World Ministries reports stunning growth in the church among Muslim populations. Two decades ago in Mauritania, there were no known believers or church groups. In 1999 there were around 100 Christians in 4 or 5 groups. Morocco has gone from 300 believers in 8 to 10 groups two decades ago to 900 in 20 to 25. Algeria, site of a civil war that has killed tens of thousands of people, has seen the church grow from 1,200 believers in 12 to 18 church groups to 12,000 Christians in 60 to 80 groups. Tunisia has grown from 30 believers in two or three groups to 150 in five or six. Even Libya, with no believers or groups 20 years ago, now has 8 to 10 evangelical believers.[20]

Indonesia, the world's largest Muslim nation, has seen periodic outbreaks of violence against its Christian minority. The economic crisis and government instability have given a green light to radicals seeking to settle old scores. Churches have been burned down and Christians murdered; at least 500 Christians in Ambon were murdered in 1999, and hundreds more perished in the year 2000. (Not all could be classified as martyrs for their faith, however, as the violence there is sometimes mutual.) Yet some church leaders report a strong revival that has been powering church growth over the last five years. Nus Reimas of the Indonesian Evangelical Alliance says that some believe the country's Christian community numbers around 20 million people, significantly higher than the official estimate of 13 to 15 million.

"We need lots of support and prayer, because the doors are really open right now in this country," Reimas said.[21]

The church is growing amid persecution elsewhere, too. In China, Christians have been among those jailed and fined heavily by authorities for engaging in illegal religious activities. Yet church growth continues, although its extent is unknown. Estimates of the size of the house church movement range anywhere from 8 million to 80 or 90 million, again showing how hype can quickly fill in the gaps of missing data. A more solid guess might be around 30 million, compared to about 5 million Protestants and Catholics combined in 1949.

In Sri Lanka, which is mostly Buddhist, Christians have been derided as tools of colonialism since the 1960s. Lately, however, they have been targeted by extremists because of their evangelistic success. Amid the brutal civil war between Buddhist and Hindu partisans, lay Christians have carried the gospel to almost every village. New Christians "come from almost all walks of life, including Buddhists, Hindus, village leaders, businessmen, farmers, and housewives," reported Charles R. A. Hoole of Colombo Theological Seminary.[22]

The role of the cross

Some missions leaders stress that hazardous duty has always been, and should continue to be, accepted as part of the cost of doing the Lord's business around the world. The path to glory runs past the cross. Concerning his own death, the Lord said that "unless a kernel of wheat falls into the ground and dies, it remains only a single seed. But if it dies, it produces many seeds" (John 12:24). The Apostle Paul reminds us that since Christ lowered himself to an ignominious death on a Roman cross, "Therefore God exalted him to the highest place" (Phil. 2:9a). What glory may we rob from overseas Christians if we, out of compassion and righteous anger, always keep them safe with government power?

While the newly heightened awareness of persecution is largely good, Western Christians who are tempted to eradicate it by political means may be forgetting church and missions history.

It is good and right to stand against evil, but how we do it can make all the difference.

FURTHER READING

Annual "World Watch List" (Santa Ana: Open Doors with Brother Andrew).

Their Blood Cries Out, by Paul Marshall, with Lela Gilbert (Dallas: Word, 1997).

Handbook on Religious Liberty Around the World, edited by Pedro C. Moreno (Charlottesville: Rutherford Institute, 1996).

In the Lion's Den: A Primer on Mounting Persecution and How American Christians Can Respond (Anderson, Ind.: Bristol House, 1996).

"Hedging our bets," by Ralph Covell, *EMQ*, April 1994.

"Toward a theology of evacuation," by Bradley N. Hill, *EMQ*, July 2000.

DISCUSSION QUESTIONS

1. *What are some of the factors that have led to an increase in public concern about religious liberty?*

2. *What avenues of response are available in the battle against persecution?*

3. *What are some of the pros and cons of asking the government to step in?*

4. *What are some of the spiritual benefits of persecution?*

5. *Do you think persecution should always be stopped, even when the church is growing?*

Part V
CONCLUSION

Chapter 22

What's Next?

Sierra Leone has become a foretaste of hell for hundreds of thousands trapped in the West African nation's gruesome civil war. Although the fighting officially ended in July 1999, atrocities continue in some areas. Half of Sierra Leone's people have been displaced, and the country has the world's worst child mortality rate. Perhaps as many as 3,000 people have had limbs randomly hacked off.

In one camp for amputees, Moktar, a member of Sierra Leone's Muslim majority, heard from Christians about Jesus' command to forgive those who persecute and abuse you. Moktar decided that he would forgive those who had sliced off his right arm and ear. Then he met the man who had tied him down, along with the one who did the cutting. Their consciences stricken, they offered Moktar money to compensate him for his loss. Moktar refused. Instead of perpetuating the cycle of violence and vengeance, however, Moktar simply forgave them. Clive Calver, president of World Relief, added, "Now Moktar wants to find the Jesus who has given him that strength."[1]

Taking the long view?

The great missionary statesman John R. Mott coined the phrase "The evangelization of the world in this generation." That was at the start of the 20th century, when Western (and Christian) optimism believed anything was possible. That optimism was followed by two devastating world wars, theological liberalism, unparalleled prosperity in the West, the re-emergence of the globe's great non-Western religions, the emergence and collapse of Soviet communism, the re-igniting of tribal hatreds and chaos, and the promise and perils of technology. At the beginning of the 21st century, certainty has been replaced by uncertainty. Can Christ's Great Commission still be accomplished? And, if so, when?

Jay Gary, who directs the Christian Futures Network in Colorado Springs, says the critical first step to completing the Great Commission is a dose of courageous realism at home – "the courage of mission leadership to recognize that it has propagated a scandal of evangelization in raising the rhetoric of closure without changing [its] field deployment priorities among the unreached."[2]

The year 2000, rather than being seen as simply the latest sign of missions failure from a church that seemingly is better at concocting grandiose plans than doing the gritty work of evangelism, should perhaps be seen as a new launch point. Gary says we need to take the long view: "To finish evangelizing the 25 percent of world population which remains unevangelized will likely take two or three generations. I am talking here of awareness and access to the gospel. The task will be completed as much through increasing internationalization, opening of shared markets, as it will be through missionary efforts."[3]

Gary, author of *The Star of 2000* and consultation director of GCOWE 2000 in 1989, predicts "a revolution in our understanding of the Great Commission ... from a closed view of history to an open view of history... .Within 20 years, the 'already, not yet' consensus could shift to an 'already, much more' theology. So instead of asking, 'What is the key to completing the Great Commission in our lifetimes, we will likely ask ... , 'What is the key to global transformation?'"[4]

Missions thinkers interviewed for this book indicate that those seeking to finish the missions task must acknowledge that it is likely to be a tough and tortuous job. Gary says that while it will probably take only two or three more generations to evangelize the 25 percent of the world's population without access to the gospel, making disciples will take far longer.

"The emergence of indigenous and growing churches among the 4,000 remaining unreached peoples will take longer," he said. "It will take a combination of factors, such as pluralism and intercivilizational dialogues, plus missionary deployment, to see long-term changes emerge. This is an area where those who sow may never know those who reap. By the year 2033, we will realize that we must measure our progress in world missions by centuries, not just decades."[5]

Such talk is bitter medicine to Christians who believed in A.D. 2000 as a terminus or who still believe that the completion of the Great Commission is around the next corner. The danger is that many who have been sprinting toward what they see as the finish line may give up with the realization that they are in a grueling marathon. Such disobedience, however, would not only belittle Christ, who bought our salvation on the cross, but also mock the bravery of all who have gone before us in centuries past to share the gospel.

As the writer of Hebrews said, "Therefore, since we are surrounded by such a great cloud of witnesses, let us throw off everything that hinders and the sin that so easily entangles, and let us run with perseverance the race marked out for us. Let us fix our eyes on Jesus, the author and perfecter of our faith, who for the joy set before him endured the cross, scorning its shame, and sat down at the right hand of the throne of God. Consider him who endured such opposition from sinful men, so that you will not grow weary and lose heart" (Heb. 12:1–2).

I believe that much work remains before the church, in the authority of Christ, will have made disciples of all nations and her Lord will return (Matt. 28:16–20). However, an abiding belief of the church has been the imminent return of Christ, meaning that he could come at any time. As the resurrected Jesus told the disciples just before his ascension, "It is not for you to know the times or dates the Father has set by his own authority. But you will receive power when the Holy Spirit comes on you, and you will be my witnesses in Jerusalem, and in all Judea and Samaria, and to the ends of the earth" (Acts 1:7–8).

Millennium minefields

Looking into the future, absent divine revelation, is perilous business. While some late 20th-century trends in world missions will undoubtedly continue, others will emerge, unlooked for and unplanned for. Who, after all, predicted the sudden collapse of the Soviet Union? The Internet explosion? The Asian financial crisis? Dolly, the cloned sheep?

Secular seers agree that the electronic information revolution of the '90s will continue but will morph into new forms with unanticipated consequences. The Internet, for example, is eroding the information hegemony long enjoyed by dictatorships as disparate as China's and Saudi Arabia's. Such technology can be a double-edged microchip for missions, however. While previously restricted nations may now have the opportunity to hear the gospel through electronic means, they also are being exposed to the computer-enhanced images of a global culture focused mainly on materialism, not the deep questions of life.

Paul Borthwick points out that while technology makes completing the Great Commission possible, it has also brought about "a corresponding information overload resulting in complacency in the North American church."[6]

David Hesselgrave, echoing Kenneth Kantzer, says he is tempted to be a short-term pessimist but a long-term optimist. "If the futurologists I have read are correct, 21st-century missionaries will inherit a challenging and even chaotic world," he said. "But natural disasters, social upheaval, moral decline, and religious confusion entail opportunities to demonstrate concern, togetherness, holiness, and commitment. The new century will probably not be to our liking. But it will certainly present tremendous opportunities to demonstrate the truth and power of Christ."[7]

As noted in chapter 15, the flip side, though, may be a temptation to broaden, and thus weaken, the missionary mandate. Noting that mission is increasingly understood as holistic – "inclusive of a wide variety of ameliorative humanitarian, social, and even political efforts" – since the Lausanne conference in 1974, Hesselgrave fears that the priority task of proclamation risks being marginalized.

Another missiological minefield is the current postmodern theological climate (see chapter 5). A culture of tolerance and the increasingly common experience of rubbing shoulders with decent, hard-working Hindus and Buddhists cause some evangelicals to question old biblical certainties about judgment and the afterlife. What happens to all those who, through no fault of their own, never hear of God's offer of salvation in Christ? What of Muslims who are said to be doing their best to follow the "God" they know? Isn't Allah just a murky version of the God of Abraham, Isaac, and Jacob? Does divine punishment consist of eternal separation from God in hell, or annihilation?

Strategic issues

Some of the trends expected to continue into the new millennium relate to missions mobilization. Western financial assistance to non-Western movements (chapters 2, 11) is likely to continue as long as the West continues to be the wealthiest world region. While noting that such arrangements can be highly effective in terms of costs and cultural understanding, observers, such as Borthwick of Development Associates International, point to the risks of financial dependency on the part of non-Westerners and complacency on the part of Western givers.

Borthwick applauds the expanding global force, but he also notes some of its drawbacks. "Some non-Western missionaries have launched out with great zeal, but they are repeating the same mistakes as Western missionaries of 100 years ago, creating, in effect, a new generation of cultural imperialists," he says. "In addition, the romanticization of the non-Western missionary in the minds of the Western church has resulted in two dangerous trends – first, . . . that our Great Commission responsibility is over with the exception of sending money, and, second, . . . unhealthy dependency in the non-Western church."[8]

Robertson McQuilkin, who has spoken of the dangers of Westerners sending money to non-Western missionaries, asks: "Given the rise of the younger churches' missionary movement since Lausanne, will we find a way for wealthy churches to partner with poor churches without grave spiritual damage to both?"[9]

Ken Mulholland, dean and professor of missions and ministry studies at Columbia Biblical Seminary and School of Missions, notes, "Church involvement and ownership have increased dramatically. More churches, especially the megachurches, by-pass the historic agencies, but they reinvent the wheel, fail to provide adequate training and supervision, and hinder co-ordinated efforts on the field because of the radical independence of their missionary force."[10]

Hesselgrave says there is profound ambiguity concerning the new mission board and church involvement. "On the one hand, one can only applaud the rising tide of missionary vision and involvement on the part of local churches," he stated. "On the other hand, more and more missionaries are short term and 'nonprofessional' – leading to what Ralph Winter has called the 'amateurization' of Christian mission. The growth in mission boards and church involvement has not been matched by a commensurate growth in the understanding of either the mission or the church."[11]

Back to the book

Perhaps that's because the Bible has also been neglected. Recent trends in biblical theology, study of the Old Testament, and "storying" the gospel (see chapter 15), however, hint that the Bible is poised to make a comeback in missions and perhaps curb some of the worst excesses of managerial missiology.

William Dyrness, a professor at Fuller Theological Seminary in Pasadena, California, states, "I will argue . . . that it is Scripture, and not its 'message,' that is finally transcultural. . . . Although it will surely relate in some way to Christ and his work, what is transcultural is not some core truth, but Scripture – the full biblical context of Christ's work. It is this that must be allowed to strike its own spark in the light of the needs of particular cultures."[12]

Hesselgrave approves of the trend. "It seems apparent that, as we enter a new century and a new millennium in the history of the Christian church and its mission, God the Holy Spirit is using leading theologians, missiologists, Bible scholars and practitioners to speak with one voice," he said. "Communication strategy may dictate an emphasis on certain felt needs, cultural themes, current issues or particular verses as 'entering wedges.' But the 'big story' that unfolds from Creation in Genesis to Christ in the Gospels to the Kingdom in Revelation is crucial to Great Commission missionizing . . . as we enter a new century in missions God is calling us back to Scripture itself – not just to its plenary authority but also to its proper use."[13]

If the Scriptures say anything about what constitutes obedience to the Great Commission, they say Christ's followers are, at a minimum, to "make disciples" (Matt. 28:19). For missionaries and overseas Christians to make a lasting impact in the 21st century, they will have to give up splashy but ineffective campaigns and refocus their efforts on the essentials of the faith.

"Make disciples, not converts," Borthwick advised. "We have emphasized the making of evangelical-experience converts, which has at times resulted in an anemic church and in nominal Christians."[14]

McQuilkin says home churches will need to be disciples themselves: "The key to completing the Great Commission is the energizing power of the Holy Spirit, but the key to unleashing that power is obedient faith, and I'm not all that confident the American church is connecting with him on those terms."[15]

Yet the Age of Uncertainty vanishes for every Christian who believes and obeys God's Word. In every Sierra Leone, God is working in the hearts of people like Moktar, drawing them to himself. The church needs to recapture a biblical understanding of God and its own role so that it can, in the phrasing of William Carey, "expect great things from God" and "attempt great things for God."

While the hope of a Year 2000 finish may be gone, the church will always need an eschatological perspective, a vision of the end, so that it will know how to live in the present. The Apostle Peter had a truly biblical view of life as he awaited the Day of the Lord, when the present heavens and earth will be consumed by fire: "Since everything will be destroyed in this way, what kind of people ought you to be? You ought to live holy and godly lives as you look forward to the day of God and speed its coming. But in keeping with his promise we are looking forward to a new heaven and a new earth, the home of righteousness" (2 Pet. 3:11–13).

FURTHER READING

With an Eye on the Future: Development and Mission in the 21st Century, edited by Duane Elmer (Monrovia: MARC, 1996).

Mustard Seed Versus McWorld: Reinventing Life and Faith for the Future, by Tom Sine (Grand Rapids: Baker Books, 1999).

Mission at the Dawn of the 21st Century: A Vision for the Church, edited by Paul Varo Martinson and Fredrik A. Schiotz (Minneapolis: Kirk House Publishers, 1999).

The Church Is Bigger Than You Think: Structures and Strategies for the Church in the 21st Century, by Patrick Johnstone (Fort Washington: Christian Focus Publications/WEC International, 1998).

Changing the Mind of Missions, by James F. Engel and William A. Dyrness (Downers Grove: InterVarsity Press, 2000).

DISCUSSION QUESTIONS

1. *What signs in this book give you hope that the Great Commission to make disciples of all nations can be completed? When might this happen?*

2. *What are some of the key challenges facing the evangelical missions movement at the beginning of the third millennium?*

3. *How can the Bible be made central to all we do in missions?*

4. *What one or two things can you or your group do to become more effective and faithful in world missions in the 21st century?*

Appendix

Essential Missions Resources

Periodicals

East–West Church & Ministry Report
4 issues per year; $44.95 USA and Canada,
$54.95 international, $19.95 e-mail.
Missions and church trends in the former Soviet Union and
Central Europe.
The Global Center, Beeson Divinity School, Samford
University, Box 292268, Birmingham, AL 35229.

Evangelical Missions Quarterly
4 issues per year; $21.95.
A professional journal offering practical help for missionaries,
mission executives, and churches.
Evangelism and Missions Information Service, P.O. Box 794,
Wheaton, ILL 60189.

Great Commission Handbook
1 issue per year; $5.
Ministry opportunities, educational options, and more.
REAL Media, P.O. Box 3550, Barrington, ILL 60011–9975.

International Bulletin of Missionary Research
4 issues per year; $21.
Academic look at history, biographies, and issues.
Overseas Ministries Study Center, 490 Prospect St., New
Haven, CT 06511.

Mission Frontiers
6 issues per year, by donation.
Trends, commentary, and more.
US Center for World Mission, 1605 E. Elizabeth St., Pasadena,
CA 91104.

World Christian
4 issues per year; $14.95.
Popular look at trends, ministry opportunities, and news.
World In Need Press, P.O. Box 1525, Oak Park, ILL 30304.

World Pulse
24 issues per year; $29.95.
The premier newsletter of trends, features, interviews, and
current events.
Evangelism and Missions Information Service, P.O. Box 794,
Wheaton, ILL 60189.

Books

Biographical Dictionary of Christian Missions.
Edited by Gerald Anderson.
Wm. B. Eerdmans Publishing Co., 255 Jefferson Ave. S.E.,
Grand Rapids, MI 49503, 1999, 845 pp; $50.

Bosch, David J., *Transforming Mission: Paradigm Shifts in
Theology of Mission.*
Orbis Books, Orbis Books, P.O. Box 302, Maryknoll, NY
10545–0302, 1991, 587 pp; $25.

*Directory of Schools and Professors of Mission and
Evangelism (1999–2001).*
Edited by John A. Siewert and Dotsey Welliver. Evangelism
and Missions Information Service, P.O. Box 794, Wheaton,
ILL 60189, 1999, 218 pp; $17.95.

Evangelical Dictionary of World Missions.
Edited by A. Scott Moreau. Baker Books, P.O. Box 6287,
Grand Rapids, MI 49516–6287, 2000, 1,168 pp; $60.

Johnstone, Patrick, *The Church is Bigger Than You Think:*
The Unfinished Task of World Evangelisation.
Christian Focus Publications, Geanies House, Fern,
Ross-shire, IV20 1TW, Great Britain; and WEC, Bulstrode,
Gerrards Cross, Bucks, Great Britain, SL9 8SZ, 1998, 314 pp;
£9.99.

Johnstone, Patrick, *Operation World: The Day-by-Day Guide*
To Praying for the World.
OM Publishing, P.O. Box 300, Carlisle, UK CA3 0QS, 1993,
662 pp; $14.99. (Sixth edition due in 2001.)

Mission Handbook 1998–2000. 17th ed.
Edited by John A. Siewert and Edna G. Valdez. MARC,
800 W. Chestnut Ave., Monrovia, Ca. 81016–3198, 1997,
512 pp; $49.95. (2001–2003, 18th edition, edited by John A.
Siewert and Dotsey Welliver, soon to be available from the
Evangelism and Missions Information Service, P.O. Box 794,
Wheaton, ILL 60189.)

Perspectives on the World Christian Movement: A Reader.
Rev. ed.
Edited by Ralph D. Winter and Steven C. Hawthorne. William
Carey Library, P.O. Box 40129, Pasadena, CA 91114; and
Paternoster, P.O. Box 300, Kingstown Broadway, Carlisle, UK
CA3 0QS, 1981, 1992, 944 pp; $17.95. (Smaller, 782-page
1999 third edition available for $25.99.)

Tucker, Ruth A., *From Jerusalem to Irian Jaya:*
A Biographical History of Christian Missions.
Zondervan Books, 5300 Patterson Ave. S.E., Grand Rapids,
MI 49530, 1983, 512 pp; $24.99.

Organizations

Many more are listed in the *Mission Handbook* (see p. 202).

Advancing Churches in Missions Commitment
4201 North Peachtree Road, Suite 300, Atlanta,
GA 30341. Call (404) 237–2585.
E-mail: 76331.2051@compuserve.com

Association of Evangelical Relief and Development
Organizations
220 I St., N.E., Suite 270, Washington, DC 20002.
Call (202) 547–3743. E-mail: sduss@worldvision.org

Association of International Mission Services, for charismatic-
oriented agencies
P.O. Box 64534, Virginia Beach, VA 23464.
Call (757) 579–5850. E-mail: AIMS@cbn.org

Billy Graham Center
Wheaton College, Wheaton, ILL 60187–5593.
Call (630) 752–5157. Web: www.wheaton.edu/bgc

Coalition in Support of Indigenous Ministries
c/o EFMA, 4201 North Peachtree Road, Suite 300,
Atlanta, GA 30341. Call Daniel Rickett at (509) 343–4038.
E-mail: DanielRickett@compuserve.com

Evangelical Fellowship of Mission Agencies
4201 North Peachtree Road, Suite 300, Atlanta, GA 30341.
Call (404) 457–6677. E-mail: EFMA@xc.org

Evangelical Missiological Society
P.O. Box 794, Wheaton, ILL 60189. Call Ken Mulholland at
(803) 754–4100 for details about membership and
publications. E-mail: Kenm@ciu.edu
The EMS publishes annual volumes, which are available from
William Carey Library (see p. 204).

Evangelism and Missions Information Service of the Billy
Graham Center at Wheaton College (publisher of *World
Pulse, Evangelical Missions Quarterly*,
and numerous missions books), P.O. Box 794, Wheaton, ILL
60189. Call (630) 752–7158. E-mail: emis@wheaton.edu

Interdenominational Foreign Mission Association
P.O. Box 398, Wheaton, ILL 60189. Call (630) 682–9270.
E-mail: IFMA@aol.com

United States Center for World Mission, 1605 E. Elizabeth St.,
Pasadena, CA 91104. Call (626) 797–1111.
Web: www.uscwm.org

William Carey Library
Publisher and distributor of many missions titles.
P.O. Box 40129, Pasadena, CA 91114. Call (626) 798–0819.
E-mail: orders@wclbooks.com

World Evangelical Fellowship North American Office
P.O. Box WEF, Wheaton, ILL 60189–8004.
Call (630) 668–0440.
E-mail: WEF-NA@xc.org

World Relief Corp. (the assistance arm of the National
Association of Evangelicals, USA)
P.O. Box WRC, Wheaton, ILL 60189. Call (630) 665–0235.
E-mail: WorldRelief@xc.org

World Vision Publications (formerly MARC, publisher
and distributor of many titles on missions and holism)
800 W. Chestnut Ave., Monrovia, CA 91016–3198.
Call (626) 301–7720.
Web: www.marcpublications.com

Education

Perspectives on the World Christian Movement
Based on the book of the same name; a course for church lay
people on the history, theology, and practice of world
missions.
US Center for World Mission, 1605 E. Elizabeth St., Pasadena,
CA 91114. Call (626) 797–1111. Web: www.perspectives.org

Notes

INTRODUCTION

1. Quoted in Stan Guthrie, "Thus spake Jesus," *Evangelical Missions Quarterly*, July 1999, pp. 344–8.
2. See <www.ad2000.org> for more and updated information.
3. Quoted by Stan Guthrie, "Mission possible," *New Man*, June 1997, p. 49.
4. David B. Barrett and Todd M. Johnson, "Status of global mission, AD 2000, in context of 20th and 21st centuries," *International Bulletin of Missionary Research*, January 2000, p. 25.
5. Guthrie, "Mission Possible," p. 49.
6. Will Norton, Sr., "A.D. 2000: In retrospect and prospect," *World Pulse*, 7 January 2000, p. 2.

CHAPTER 1

1. Samuel F. Metcalf, "When local churches act like agencies," *EMQ*, April 1993, p. 142.
2. Deann Alford, "The right stuff," *World Pulse*, 21 August 1999, p. 1.
3. Alford, "The right stuff," p. 2.
4. John A. Siewert, "Growing local church initiatives," *Mission Handbook 1998–2000* (Pasadena: Mission Advanced Research and Communication Center (MARC), 1997), p. 59.
5. Tom Steller, interviewed by author via Internet, 11 November 1999.
6. *Askamissionary Newsletter* (see <http://www.askamissionary.com>; send an e-mail with the word "subscribe" in the message area to <askamissionary@xc.org>).

7 Jim Reapsome, "Pulling together," *World Pulse*, 3 December 1999, p. 8.

8 Paul A. Beals, "The triad for Century 21," Evangelical Missiological Society, *Occasional Bulletin*, Spring 1999, p. 1.

9 Alford, "The right stuff," pp. 1–2.

10 Alford, "The right stuff," p. 1.

11 Tom Steller, interview by author via Internet, 11 November 1999.

CHAPTER 2

1 Jim Lo, "I tried paying national workers," *EMQ*, January 1999, pp. 14–16.

2 Chuck Bennett, "The problem with success," *EMQ*, January 1996, p. 20.

3 Patrick Johnstone, *Operation World* (Grand Rapids: Zondervan, 1993), pp. 25–6.

4 Bennett, "The problem with success," p. 21.

5 Terry Dryden, "Just one of eleven thousand," *Send!*, September/October 1999, p. 8.

6 Stan Guthrie, "New partners, new roles," *Moody*, November/December 1996, p. 2.

7 Lewis Codington, "National workers," *EMQ*, January 2000, p. 10.

8 Stan Guthrie, "Looking under the hood of the non-Western missions movement," *EMQ*, January 1995, p. 88.

9 Guthrie, "Looking under the hood," pp. 88, 92.

10 Joann Hoganson, "American dollars buy trouble," *EMQ*, October 1998, pp. 393–4.

11 Codington, p. 10.

12 Robertson McQuilkin, "Stop sending money!" *Christianity Today*, 1 March 1999, p. 59.

13 Guthrie, "New partners," p. 20.

14 Codington, p. 11.

15 Stan Guthrie, "Uganda ministry brings life to an unstable region," *World Pulse*, 19 November 1999, p. 5.

16 Bennett, "The problem with success," p. 25.

CHAPTER 3

1 "We asked . . . ," *World Pulse*, 4 August 1995, p. 3. Murray is now president of Columbia International University in Columbia, S.C.

2 Jim Raymo, "Reflections on missionary malaise," *EMQ*, October 1997, pp. 442–6. See also Jim Raymo, *Marching to a Different Drummer: Rediscovering Missions in an Age of Affluence and Self-Interest* (Fort Washington: Christian Literature Crusade, 1996).

3 Barna Research Online <http://www.barna.org/cgi-bin/Main Archives.asp>.

4 John A. Siewert and Edna G. Valdez, *Mission Handbook* (Pasadena: MARC, 1997), p. 74.

5 John A. Siewert and Dotsey Welliver, *Mission Handbook* (Wheaton: Evangelism and Missions Information Service, 2000).

6 Paul McKaughan, interview by author via Internet, 29 April 2000.

7 Gustav Niebuhr, "Churchgoers are putting smaller portion of their incomes into collection plates," *Wall Street Journal*, 31 July 1992.

8 R. Mark Dillon, "The ministry of fundraising," Wheaton College, n.d., p. 2.

9 Dillon, p. 2.

10 Dawn Rutan, "Missions on the edge of a new century: an interview with James Reapsome," *Advent Christian Witness*, June 1997, p. 9.

11 Siewert and Valdez, p. 74. See also Scott Moreau's chapter in Siewert and Welliver's 2001–2003 *Handbook*, "Putting the survey in perspective."

12 Jeremy Funk, "Organizations seek to combine evangelism with development," *World Pulse*, 23 July 1999, p. 5.

13 "We asked . . . ," p. 3.

14 "We asked . . . ," p. 3.

15 David B. Barrett and Todd M. Johnson, "Status of global mission, AD 2000, in context of 20th and 21st centuries," *International Bulletin of Missionary Research*, January 2000, p. 25.

16 Raymo, "Reflections on missionary malaise," p. 443.

17 For a discussion on this topic, see Jim Reapsome, "Do families still fit in missions?" *Final Analysis: A Decade of Commentary on the Church and World Missions* (Wheaton: Evangelism and Missions Information Service, 1999), pp. 214–16.

18 Ted Ward, "The case of the disappearing missionaries: reflections on missionary recruitment and retention," *Trinity World Forum*, Fall 1995, p. 2.

19 Raymo, "Reflections on missionary malaise," p. 444.

20 Ruth A. Tucker, *From Jerusalem to Irian Jaya* (Grand Rapids: Zondervan, 1983), p. 114.

21 Timothy George, "The faithful witness of William Carey," *EMQ*, October 1992, pp. 350–58.

CHAPTER 4

1 H. Miriam Ross, "What about Dorothy?" *EMQ*, October 1992, pp. 360–62.

2 Stan Guthrie, "Just saying No," *EMQ*, April 1998, p. 218.

3 Stan Guthrie, "Looking under the hood of the non-Western missions movement," *EMQ*, January 1995, p. 92.

4 William D. Taylor, editor, *Too Valuable to Lose: Exploring the Causes and Cures of Missionary Attrition* (Pasadena: William Carey Library, 1997). See also Jim Reapsome, "Missionary attrition," *EMQ*, April 1998, pp. 226–7.

5 Julia Flynn, "E-Mail, cellphones and frequent-flier miles let 'virtual' expats work abroad but live at home," *Wall Street Journal*, 25 October 1999, p. A26.

6 Jim Reapsome, "The day the missionary cried," *Final Analysis: A Decade of Commentary on the Church and World Missions* (Wheaton: Evangelism and Missions Information Service, 1999), pp. 123–5.

7 "What happens if . . . ," *InterCom*, September–December 1999, p. 1.

8 Kelly and Michèle O'Donnell, "The increasing scope of 'member care,'" *EMQ*, October 1990, pp. 424–8.

9 Kevin B. Rasmusen, "Partners in pain," *World Pulse*, 19 February 1999, p. 4. See also Tricia Andrews, "Team player," *World Pulse*, 19 March 1999, p. 4.

10 Janet Blomberg and Joyce Bowers, "Maturing 'missionary kid' movement is coming of age," *World Pulse*, 15 May 1998, pp. 1–2.

11 Tom Steller, interview by author via Internet, 11 November 1999.

12 Brent Lindquist, "Remember the context," *EMQ*, January 2000, p. 71.

13 Tom Steller, interview by author via Internet, 11 November 1999.

CHAPTER 5

1 Ruth A. Tucker, *From Jerusalem to Irian Jaya* (Grand Rapids: Zondervan, 1983), pp. 176–85.

2 Tucker, p. 148.

3 John Orme, "Crossing the Y2K time barrier," *IFMA News*, Winter 1999, p. 3.

4 Ronald H. Nash, *Is Jesus the Only Savior?* (Grand Rapids: Zondervan, 1994).

5 Larry Dixon, *The Other Side of the Good News* (Wheaton: Victor Books, 1992).

6 J.N.D. Anderson, *Christianity and Comparative Religion* (Downers Grove: InterVarsity Press, 1970), pp. 102–11.

7 Gregory Boyd, *God at War: The Bible and Spiritual Conflict* (Downers Grove: InterVarsity Press, 1997), p. 395.

8 Quoted by David Howard, "Crucial Questions About Hell" (review), *EMQ*, January 1995, p. 102.

9 Dawn Rutan, "Missions on the edge of a new century: an interview with James Reapsome," *Advent Christian Witness*, June 1997, p. 9.

10 James Davison Hunter, *Evangelicalism: The Coming Generation* (Chicago: The University of Chicago Press, 1987), p. 35.

11 Nash, p. 107.

12 Barna Research Online <http://www.barna.org/cgi-bin/Main Archives.asp>.

13 Nash, pp. 108–9.

14 Nash, pp. 122–3, 129.

15 Hunter, pp. 34–5.

16 Mark S. Freedman and Maxine Cohen, "Baptists' conversion deceit," *Wall Street Journal*, 30 September 1999.

17 Steve Kloehn, "Clergy ask Baptists to rethink area blitz," *Chicago Tribune*, 30 November 1999 (via Internet).

18 John Piper, *Let the Nations Be Glad! The Supremacy of God in Missions* (Grand Rapids: Baker, 1993), p. 11.

19 Robertson McQuilkin, interview by author via Internet, 17 August 1999.

20 Orme, p. 3.

21 Jim Raymo, "Reflections on missionary malaise," *EMQ*, October 1997, p. 444.

CHAPTER 6

1 David Miller, *The Lord of Bellavista* (London: Triangle, SPCK, 1998), pp. 79–84.

2 Annette Vasulka, "Cell church," *World Pulse*, 7 August 1998, p. 2.

3 John Orme, IFMA executive director, interview by author, 4 February 2000.

4 "IFMA statistical report as of December 31, 1998," p. 4. IFMA, P.O. Box 398, Wheaton, Ill. 60189.

5 Jim Reapsome, *Final Analysis: A Decade of Commentary on the Church and World Missions* (Wheaton: Evangelism and Missions Information Service, 1999), p. 208.

6 Laurel A. Cocks, "Women in mission," *EMQ*, April 1998, p. 139.

7 Gary Corwin, "Women in mission," *EMQ*, October 1997, p. 400.

8 Susan Perlman, interview by author via Internet, 4 February 2000.

9 Karen F. Carr, interview by author via Internet, 6 December 1999.

10 Perlman, *op. cit.*

11 Clark H. Pinnock, *Biblical Revelation: The Foundation of Christian Theology* (Phillipsburg: Presbyterian and Reformed Publishing Company, 1971, 1982), p. 35.

12 Perlman, *op. cit.*

13 Orme, *op. cit.*

14 Janey L. DeMeo, interview by author via Internet, 2 December 1999.

15 Cheryl Johnson Barton, interview by author via Internet, 2 December 1999.

16 Barbara Crossette, "Unicef opens global drive to halt killings of women," *New York Times*, 9 March 2000 (via Internet).

17 Stan Guthrie, "Africa: The light continent?" *World Pulse*, 19 January 1996, p. 2.

18 Barton, *op. cit.*

19 "Recognizing God's purpose for gender distinctives in marriage and family life, church and society," *Evangelical Review of Theology*, January 1997, pp. 33–7.

20 "Recognizing God's purpose," p. 37.

21 Corwin, p. 400.

CHAPTER 7

1 Frank M. Severn, "Some thoughts on the meaning of 'all nations,'" *EMQ*, October 1997, pp. 412–14.

2 Justin Long, "'Researcher' responds," *EMQ*, April 1998, p. 141.

3 Luis Bush, "Getting to the core of the core: the 10/40 Window," *Chinese in North America*, January–February 1991, p. 3.

4 Figures cited by Ted Yamamori of Food for the Hungry in Jeremy Funk, "Organizations seek to combine evangelism with development," *World Pulse*, 23 July 1999, p. 5.

5 "Getting to the core of the core," pp. 6, 8.

6 Eric Watt, "Straightline for September 1999," <AD2000@xc.org>.

7 Luis Bush, "The Brazilian church mobilizes for the 10/40 Window," September 1999, <AD2000@xc.org>.

8 Beverly Nickles, "Repentance, realism mark GCOWE '97," *World Pulse*, 1 August 1997, p. 4.

9 "Getting to the core of the core," p. 7.

10 Patrick Johnstone, *Operation World* (Grand Rapids: Zondervan, 1993), p. 57.

11 "A conversation on the Net," *EMQ*, October 1997, p. 417.

12 Stan Guthrie, "Sticks and stones: Christians in India examine role of rhetoric in persecution," *EMQ*, October 1999, pp. 468–77.

CHAPTER 8

1 Stan Guthrie, "Mission possible," *New Man*, June 1997, pp. 47–8.

2 Guthrie, p. 49.

3 "'Light at the end of the tunnel,'" *World Pulse*, 4 February 1994, p. 1.

4 Guthrie, p. 49, from interview of Johnstone via Internet, 1997.

5 Ralph D. Winter, "The new Macedonia: a revolutionary new era in mission begins," *Perspectives on the World Christian Movement: A Reader* (Pasadena: William Carey Library, 1981), pp. 293–311.

6 Justin Long, "Megatrend 9: 50 new global plans for world evangelization per year," *Monday Morning Reality Check*, 12 November 1996, <reality-check@xc.org>.

7 Guthrie, p. 49.

8 David Neff, "Stepping on toes," *World Pulse*, 17 December 1999, pp. 1–2.

9 "21 more languages now have the Bible," *UBS World Report* 349, March 2000, pp. 3–4.

10 "Peering into the next century," Trans World Radio News Release, 10 September 1999; Guthrie, p. 49.

11 James F. Engel, "Will the Great Commission become the great ad campaign?" *Christianity Today*, 26 April 1993, p. 27.

12 Paul Borthwick, interview by author via Internet, 17 August 1999.

13 Guthrie, p. 48.

14 Robertson McQuilkin, "Six inflammatory questions," *EMQ*, April 1994, pp. 130–31.

15 Jay Gary, "A church for every people – beyond 2000," *EMQ*, July 1996, pp. 293–4.

16 David J. Hesselgrave, "Inter*View*," *World Pulse*, 7 January 2000, p. 5.

17 Guthrie, p. 49.

CHAPTER 9

1 Jane Lampman, "Targeting cities with 'spiritual mapping,' prayer," *The Christian Science Monitor*, 23 September 1999, <www.csmonitor.com/durable/1999/09/23/fp15s1-csm.shtml>.

2 Patrick Johnstone, "Biblical intercession: spiritual power to change our world," *Spiritual Power and Missions: Raising the Issues* (Pasadena: William Carey Library, 1995), pp. 159–60.

3 C. S. Lewis, *The Screwtape Letters* (West Chicago: Lord and King Associates, 1976), p. 17.

4 Chuck Pierce, "Transferring the wealth from the queen's domain," *Global Prayer News*, January–March 2000, p. 2.

5 C. Peter Wagner, "The 40/70 Window: a new directive of prayer," *Global Prayer News*, January–March 2000, p. 1.

6 C. Peter Wagner, undated e-mail headed "Queen." For more information, contact P.O. Box 63060, Colorado Springs, CO 80962–3060.

7 Pierce, p. 2.

8 Wagner, "The 40/70 Window," p. 12.

9 Robert J. Priest, Thomas Campbell, and Bradford A. Mullen, "Missiological syncretism: the new animistic paradigm," *Spiritual Power and Missions: Raising the Issues* (Pasadena: William Carey Library, 1995), pp. 11–12.

10 Priest, Campbell, and Mullen, p. 12.

11 Michael A. Wright, "Some observations on Thai animism," *Missionary Readings in Anthropology* (South Pasadena: William Carey Library, 1974), p. 116. Quoted by Philip Steyne in *Gods of Power: A Study of the Beliefs and Practices of Animists* (Houston: Touch Publications, 1989), p. 41.

12 Charles H. Kraft, "'Christian animism' or God-given authority?" *Spiritual Power and Missions: Raising the Issues* (Pasadena: William Carey Library, 1995), pp. 88–135.

[13] Kraft, p. 92.

[14] Charles R.A. Hoole, "Territorial spirits," *EMQ*, April 1997, p. 136.

[15] C. Peter Wagner, *Warfare Prayer* (Ventura: Regal Books, 1992), p. 19. Quoted by Mike Wakely, "A critical look at a new 'key' to evangelization," *EMQ*, April 1995, p. 158.

[16] Timothy George, "The faithful witness of William Carey," *EMQ*, October 1992, pp. 352–3.

[17] John Piper, *Let the Nations Be Glad! The Supremacy of God in Missions* (Grand Rapids: Baker Books, 1993), p. 51.

[18] John Orme, "Executive director's report," 78th IFMA Annual Meeting, 15–18 September 1995, Fort Mill, S.C., p. 5.

[19] John Piper, *The Pleasures of God* (Portland, Or.: Multnomah Press, 1991), p. 142.

[20] Piper, *The Pleasures of God*, p. 123.

[21] George Otis, Jr., *The Last of the Giants* (Tarrytown: Fleming H. Revell Company, 1991), p. 88.

[22] Wakely, p. 158.

CHAPTER 10

[1] David Wang, "Now, who is not ministering to China?" *Asian Report*, September/October 1999, p. 1.

[2] Andrew Atkins, "Work teams? No, 'taste and see' teams," *EMQ*, October 1991, p. 385.

[3] Jim Raymo, "Reflections on missionary malaise," *EMQ*, October 1997, p. 445.

[4] Jim Reapsome, "The new face of world missions," *Missionary Messenger*, December 1999, p. 3.

[5] John Maust, "Short-term missions boom: growing numbers of lay Christians take 'vacations with a purpose,' serving the church overseas," *Latin America Evangelist*, April–June 1991, p. 18.

[6] Susan G. Loobie, "Short-term missions: is it worth it?" *Latin America Evangelist*, January–March 2000, p. 7.

[7] John A. Siewert and Edna G. Valdez, *Mission Handbook 1998–2000* (Monrovia: MARC, 1997), p. 74.

[8] John A. Siewert and Dotsey Welliver, *Mission Handbook 2001–2003* (Wheaton: Evangelism and Missions Information Service, 2000).

9   Siewert and Valdez, p. 74. The numbers are roughly the same in the 2001–2003 edition.
10 Seth Barnes, "The changing face of the missionary force," *EMQ*, October 1992, p. 376.
11 James F. Engel and Jerry D. Jones, *Baby Boomers and the Future of World Missions* (Orange: Management Development Associates, 1989), p. 33.
12 Engel and Jones, p. 33.
13 Siewert and Valdez, p. 74. See also Siewert and Welliver.
14 Roger Peterson, *Is Short-Term Mission Really Worth the Time and Money?* (Minneapolis: STEM Ministries, 1991).
15 Leslie Pelt, "What's behind the wave of short-termers?" *EMQ*, October 1992, p. 385.
16 Ajith Fernando, "Some thoughts on missionary burnout," *EMQ*, October 1999, p. 442.
17 David Mays, interview by author via Internet, 17 August 1999.
18 Tom Steller, interview by author via Internet, 11 November 1999.
19 The author is a member of the Board of Missions of College Church in Wheaton, Illinois.
20 Jim Lo, "Short-term missionaries," *EMQ*, April 1997, p. 137.
21 Paul Borthwick, "5 Reasons Not to Leave the Country," *Commissioned*, Vol. XVI No. 2, pp. 16–19.
22 Jim Hogrefe, *Askamissionary Newsletter* (see <http:/www.askamissionary.com>; send an e-mail with the word "subscribe" in the message area to <askamissionary@xc.org>).
23 Atkins, p. 387.

CHAPTER 11

1   Stan Guthrie, "Children at risk: The biggest little mission field in the world?" *EMQ*, January 1998, pp. 88–94.
2   Paul Borthwick, "What local churches are saying to mission agencies," *EMQ*, July 1999, pp. 324–30.
3   John A. Siewert and Edna G. Valdez, *Mission Handbook 1998–2000* (Monrovia: MARC, 1997), pp. 61–3.
4   See David Hicks, *Globalizing Missions* (Miami: Editorial Unilit, 1994), pp. 13–15.
5   Bill Taylor, "Great Commission Global Roundtable," World Evangelical Fellowship press release, 10 November 1999, pp. 1–2.

6 "Strategic alliances in Nigeria, Korea, India," *GMI Info*, Fall/Winter 1999, p. 6.
7 "Partnership progress," *World Pulse*, 1 October 1999, p. 3.
8 Chuck Bennett, "Open letter to Robertson McQuilkin," *EMQ*, April 2000, pp. 211–12.
9 "InterView," *World Pulse*, 20 August 1999, p. 5.
10 Paul Borthwick, interview by author via Internet, 17 August 1999.
11 Walter Lawrence Brown, "A Call for a Moratorium on Sending African Theology Students to America," unpublished paper, November 1999.
12 Daniel Rickett, "Preventing dependency: developmental partnering," *EMQ*, October 1998, p. 439.

CHAPTER 12

1 Ralph D. Winter, "The new Macedonia: a revolutionary new era in mission begins," *Perspectives on the World Christian Movement: A Reader* (Pasadena: William Carey Library, 1981), pp. 293–311.
2 The Lausanne Committee, "The Willowbank Report," *Perspectives on the World Christian Movement: A Reader* (Pasadena: William Carey Library, 1981), pp. 507–38.
3 Tom Steffen, "How user-friendly is your teaching?" *EMQ*, April 1996, pp. 178–85.
4 Craig Bird (Baptist Press), "Storytelling opens Muslim ears in Togo," *EMQ*, April 1996, pp. 182–3.
5 Bruce Thomas, "The gospel for shame cultures," *EMQ*, July 1994, pp. 284–90.
6 See *EMQ*, April 1999, for several articles on the subject.
7 Tom Steffen, "Don't show the *Jesus* film . . . ," *EMQ*, July 1993, pp. 272–6.
8 Stan Guthrie, "Just saying No," *EMQ*, April 1998, p. 222.
9 Bradley Baurain, "The church that time forgot," *World Pulse*, 5 January 1996, pp. 4–5.
10 Steve Cochrane (interview), "To Do C5 or Not?" *YWAMer*, October 1999–January 2000, p. 6.
11 Stan Guthrie, "Sticks and stones," *EMQ*, October 1999, pp. 474–5.
12 Guthrie, "Just saying No," p. 222.
13 Phil Parshall, "Danger! New directions in contextualization," *EMQ*, October 1998, pp. 404–10.

14 Parshall, p. 406.
15 Guthrie, "Just saying No," p. 319.
16 "Inter*View*," *World Pulse*, 19 February 1999, p. 5.

CHAPTER 13

1 "The long, costly journey of a translation," *Alliance World Prayer Line*, January 1998, p. 1.
2 David Dougherty, "What's happening to missions mobilization?" *EMQ*, July 1998, pp. 276–7. I am indebted to Dougherty for identifying and naming the trends discussed in this chapter.
3 Dougherty, p. 278.
4 "JAARS launches short-term ministry," *World Pulse*, 21 January 2000.
5 Paul Beals, "The triad for Century 21," *Occasional Bulletin* of the Evangelical Missiological Society, Spring 1999, p. 3.
6 Christopher J. H. Wright, "Reaching the resistant: barriers and bridges for mission" (review), *EMQ*, April 2000, p. 246.
7 "Russian Ministries president named chairman of CoMission II" press release, Peter Deyneka Russian Ministries, 5 February 1997, p. 1.
8 Brad Thiessen, "Team of young adults commits to ten year mission effort" press release, MBMS International, 1 December 1999, pp. 1–2.

CHAPTER 14

1 Stan Guthrie, "Just saying No," *EMQ*, April 1998, p. 222.
2 Stan Guthrie, "Tentmaking Putting Down Stakes in Missions Movement," *Christianity Today*, 13 November 1995, p. 80.
3 Tetsunao Yamamori, "Tentmakers launch international network," *World Pulse*, 8 April 1994, p. 1.
4 Guthrie, "Tentmaking Putting Down Stakes," p. 80.
5 Guthrie, "Tentmaking Putting Down Stakes," p. 80.
6 Gary Ginter, interview by author, plus "Tentmaking Putting Down Stakes," p. 80.
7 Guthrie, "Tentmaking Putting Down Stakes," p. 80.
8 Jim Raymo, "Reflections on missionary malaise," *EMQ*, October 1997, p. 445.

⁹ Guthrie, "Tentmaking Putting Down Stakes," p. 81.

¹⁰ John A. Siewert and Edna G. Valdez, *Mission Handbook 1998–2000* (Monrovia: MARC, 1997), p. 74. See also the 2001–2003 edition published by the Evangelism and Missions Information Service, Wheaton, Ill.

¹¹ Guthrie, "Tentmaking Putting Down Stakes," p. 81.

¹² Guthrie, "Tentmaking Putting Down Stakes," p. 81.

¹³ Jonathan Lewis, *Working Your Way to the Nations* (Downers Grove: InterVarsity Press, 1997).

¹⁴ Guthrie, "Tentmaking Putting Down Stakes," p. 81.

¹⁵ Guthrie, "Tentmaking Putting Down Stakes," p. 81.

¹⁶ Guthrie, "Just saying No," p. 223.

CHAPTER 15

¹ Steve Kloehn, "Clergy ask Baptists to rethink area blitz," *Chicago Tribune*, 30 November 1999 (via Internet).

² Quoted by Isabelo Megalit, "Mission field and mission force," *East Asia's Billions*, January 2000, p. 5.

³ See David J. Hesselgrave, "Redefining holism," *EMQ*, July 1999, pp. 278–9.

⁴ Hesselgrave, p. 278.

⁵ Bryant L. Myers, "In response . . . another look at 'holistic mission,'" *EMQ*, July 1999, pp. 286–7.

⁶ Darrow L. Miller, with Stan Guthrie, *Discipling Nations: The Power of Truth to Transform Cultures* (Seattle: Youth With A Mission, 1998), p. 32.

⁷ Jeremy Funk, "Organizations seek to combine evangelism with development," *World Pulse*, 23 July 1999, p. 5.

⁸ Steven Spaulding, "Holism," *EMQ*, April 2000, p. 147.

⁹ Jay Gary, interview by author via Internet, 9 September 1999.

¹⁰ Meredith Long, "Walking with the poor," "Working with the poor," *EMQ*, April 2000, pp. 258–62.

¹¹ Ronald H. Nash, *Is Jesus the Only Savior?* (Grand Rapids: Zondervan, 1994), p. 166. See also Thomas Guterbock, "What Do Christians Expect from Christian Relief and Development?" *Stewardship Journal*, Summer/Fall 1992, p. 24.

¹² Stan Guthrie, "Welcome to A.D. 2000. Now what?" *World Pulse*, 7 January 2000, p. 6.

CHAPTER 16

1 Stan Guthrie, "Can we all just get along?" *World Pulse*, 8 March 1996, pp. 1–2.
2 Patrick Johnstone, *Operation World* (Grand Rapids: Zondervan Publishing House, 1993), p. 25.
3 Johnstone, p. 65.
4 Johnstone, p. 26.
5 David J. Hesselgrave, "Third World Mission Congress meets in Japan," *World Pulse*, 3 December 1999, pp. 1–2.
6 Quoted by Donald K. Smith, "Reviewing the place of Western missionaries for the third millennium," *EMQ*, January 1999, pp. 56–7.
7 John A. Siewert and Edna G. Valdez, *Mission Handbook 1998–2000* (Monrovia: MARC, 1997), p. 74; John A. Siewert and Dotsey Welliver, *Mission Handbook 2001–2003* (Wheaton, Ill.: Evangelism and Missions Information Service, 2000).
8 Stan Guthrie, "New Partners, New Roles," *Moody*, November/ December 1996, p. 20.
9 Stan Guthrie, "Looking under the hood of the non-Western missions movement," *EMQ*, January 1995, pp. 88–9.
10 Guthrie, "Looking under the hood," p. 95.

CHAPTER 17

1 Pedro C. Moreno, "Rapture and renewal in Latin America," *First Things*, June/July 1997, pp. 31–2.
2 Deann Alford, "Hour of power," *World Pulse*, 1 October 1999, p. 1.
3 Patrick Johnstone, *Operation World* (Grand Rapids: Zondervan Publishing House, 1993), p. 23.
4 David M. Barrett and Todd M. Johnson, "Annual statistical table on global mission: 2000," *International Bulletin of Missionary Research*, January 2000, p. 25.
5 Barrett and Johnson, p. 25.
6 David Shibley, *A Force in the Earth* (Lake Mary: Creation House, 1997), p. 25.
7 H.D. Hunter, "Charismatic movement," *Dictionary of Christianity in America* (Downers Grove: InterVarsity Press, 1990), p. 241.

[8] L. Grant McClung, Jr., "'Try to get people saved': revisiting the paradigm of an urgent Pentecostal missiology," *The Globalization of Pentecostalism: A Religion Made To Travel* (Oxford: Regnum Books International, 1999), p. 33.

[9] Hunter, pp. 243–4.

[10] "InterView," *World Pulse*, 19 March 1999, p. 5.

[11] Frank D. Macchia, "The struggle for global witness: shifting paradigms in Pentecostal theology," *The Globalization of Pentecostalism: A Religion Made To Travel* (Oxford: Regnum Books International, 1999), p. 16.

[12] Denise da Silva Maranhão, "New life for the children, Brazil," in Tetsunao Yamamori, Bryant L. Myers, C. René Padilla and Greg Rake (eds.), *Serving with the Poor in Latin America* (Monrovia: MARC, 1997), p. 40.

[13] Hunter, p. 241.

[14] "In India, trouble between beliefs," *Philadelphia Inquirer*, 23 January 2000, p. J7.

[15] Pedro C. Moreno, "Evangelical churches," *Religious Freedom and Evangelization in Latin America: The Challenge of Religious Pluralism* (Maryknoll: Orbis, 1999), p. 50.

[16] John Marcom, Jr., "The fire down south," *Forbes*, 15 October 1990, pp. 56–7.

[17] Pedro C. Moreno, "Pentecostals redefine religion in Latin America," *Wall Street Journal*, 29 August 1997, p. A11.

[18] Alford, p. 2.

[19] "Pentecostal growth in Latin America," *World Pulse*, 1 October 1999, p. 6.

[20] "Investigation reveals 'evang-elastics,'" *Latin American Ecumenical News*, July–September 1999, p. 6.

[21] Macchia, pp. 23–4.

CHAPTER 18

[1] "Once enemies, now allies," Trans World Radio press release, 5 October 1999, pp. 1–2.

[2] Ronda Oosterhoff, "Discipleship conference addresses 'superficiality' in worldwide church," *World Pulse*, 5 November 1999, p. 1.

[3] Stan Guthrie, "Evangelicals respond to unabated persecution," *EMQ*, October 1996, pp. 463–4.

4 Aggrey Mugisha, "Penetrating a paradox," *World Pulse*, 2 July 1999, p. 4.

5 Mugisha, p. 4.

6 Oosterhoff, pp. 1–2.

7 Oosterhoff, p. 2.

8 Paul Borthwick, interview by author via Internet, 17 August 1999.

9 Stan Guthrie, "Sticks and stones," *EMQ*, October 1999, pp. 475–7.

10 David Neff, "Stepping on toes," *World Pulse*, 17 December 1999, pp. 1–2.

11 From the Iguassu Affirmation, October 1999. See <www. worldevangelical.org>.

12 Joseph D'Souza, "A flaw in our recruiting strategy?" *EMQ*, April 2000, pp. 156–7.

13 J. Paul Landrey, "Trainers of Pastors International Consultation (TOPIC), Manila, 22–25 March 1999" press release, Christ for the City International, P.O. Box 241827, Omaha, Ne. 68124–5827.

14 David Miller, "Keeping trainers on track," *World Pulse*, 22 January 1999, p. 4.

15 Landrey, *op. cit.*

16 Ajith Fernando, "Some thoughts on missionary burnout," *EMQ*, October 1999, pp. 442–3.

17 Landrey, *op. cit.*

18 "Ethiopians preach in India," *World Pulse*, 2 October 1999, p. 3.

CHAPTER 19

1 Stan Guthrie, "Does global culture mark the end of missions history?" *EMQ*, July 1996, p. 328.

2 Thomas L. Friedman, *The Lexus and the Olive Tree: Understanding Globalization* (New York: Farrar, Straus & Giroux, 1999), p. 8.

3 Friedman, p. 7.

4 "The powerful idea of human rights," *New York Times*, 8 December 1999.

5 Roger Thurow, "For many Czechs, 'velvet' revolution has a coarse edge," *Wall Street Journal*, 30 November 1999, p. A1.

6 Guthrie, p. 329.

7 Toby Lester, "What is the Koran?" *The Atlantic Monthly*, January 1999, pp. 43–56.

8 Quoted by Guthrie, p. 330.

9   "Expanding radio ministry in Korea," *World Pulse*, 3 December
    1999, p. 3.
10 Guthrie, p. 330.
11 Guthrie, p. 330.
12 Guthrie, p. 331.
13 Guthrie, p. 331.
14 Guthrie, p. 332.
15 Guthrie, p. 332.
16 David Neff, "Stepping on toes," *World Pulse*, 17 December 1999,
    p. 2.
17 Guthrie, p. 333.
18 Guthrie, p. 333.
19 Guthrie, p. 334.
20 Guthrie, p. 333.
21 Guthrie, p. 334.
22 Guthrie, p. 333.
23 Guthrie, p. 333.

CHAPTER 20

1   Stan Guthrie, "Missions: Impossible?" *Moody*, November/December
    1999, pp. 46–7.
2   Thalif Deen, "Religious extremism on the rise: UN," Dawn/Inter
    Press, 8 December 1999.
3   Samuel P. Huntington, *The Clash of Civilizations and the Remaking
    of World Order* (New York: Simon & Schuster, 1996).
4   Vishal Mangalwadi, "Pope, militants and India win, liberals lose
    round one for the soul of Asia" (unpublished draft), December
    1999.
5   Nik Repkin, "Why are the unreached unreached?" *EMQ*, July 1996,
    p. 285.
6   "'Watchword in World Missions' Conference," *World Pulse*, 21 May
    1999, p. 3.
7   Stan Guthrie, "Muslim mission breakthrough," *Christianity Today*,
    13 December 1993, p. 23.
8   Stan Guthrie, "Ministries now aim to reach Hindu heads as well as
    hearts," *EMQ*, October 1997, pp. 468–9.
9   Joseph D'Souza, "Election and the new government," *India
    Communique*, November 1999, p. 1.
10 Mangalwadi, *op. cit.*

11 Mark Kelly, "Divali prayer guide" press release, International Mission Board, Southern Baptist Convention, 27 October 1999, p. 1.

12 Stan Guthrie, "Nepal: A Hindu case study," *EMQ*, October 1997, p. 473 (plus subsequent author research).

13 Guthrie, "Missions: Impossible?" p. 49.

14 Guthrie, "Missions: Impossible?" p. 49.

15 Stephen J. Glain, "EgyptAir suicide theory angers Muslims," *Wall Street Journal*, 19 November 1999, p. A18.

16 Joshua Massey, "His ways are not our ways," *EMQ*, April 1999, pp. 194–5.

17 Stan Guthrie, "Malice in the Maldives," *World Pulse*, 4 September 1998, p. 4.

18 Deann Alford, "Fighting words?" *World Pulse*, 6 November 1998, p. 1.

19 Charles R. A. Hoole, "Sri Lanka at 50," *World Pulse*, 17 April 1998, pp. 1–2.

20 Stan Guthrie, "America becoming fertile mission field for Buddhism," *Christianity Today*, 14 November 1994, p. 72.

21 Deborah Sontag, "Israel: Jewish or multicultural state?" *New York Times*, 6 December 1999 (via Internet).

22 Stan Guthrie, "Jewish evangelism getting respect it's long been denied," *EMQ*, January 1997, p. 83.

23 Joseph D'Souza, "The martyrdom of Graham Steins (*sic*) and his sons" (unpublished draft), February 1999, p. 3.

CHAPTER 21

1 Mark Kelly, "Seminary student killed, campus attacked by mob in Nigeria riots," *World Pulse*, 17 March 2000, p. 6; Mark Kelly, "Baptists bury dead, look to future after seminary attack in Nigeria," *World Pulse*, 21 April 2000, p. 7.

2 Kathi Graham, "Christians around the world unite in prayer for the persecuted church" press release, World Evangelical Fellowship, 22 November 1999, p. 1.

3 Ralph Covell, "Hedging our bets," *EMQ*, April 1994, pp. 136–9.

4 "Uzbekistan frees Christians," *World Pulse*, 1 October 1999, p. 7.

5 Stan Guthrie, "Evangelicals respond to unabated persecution," *EMQ*, October 1996, p. 462.

6 Wendy Murray Zoba, "Good news for the lost, imprisoned, abducted, and enslaved," *Christianity Today*, 9 August 1999, p. 36.

[7] "Praying for the persecuted: a direct link to the highest authority," Religious Liberty Prayer List, 10 November 1999.

[8] "Open Doors World Watch List," *World Pulse*, 18 June 1999, p. 6.

[9] Guthrie, "Evangelicals respond," p. 461.

[10] Guthrie, "Evangelicals respond," p. 462.

[11] David M. Barrett and Todd M. Johnson, "Annual statistical table on global mission: 2000," *International Bulletin of Missionary Research*, January 2000, p. 25.

[12] Guthrie, "Evangelicals respond," p. 462.

[13] Guthrie, "Evangelicals respond," pp. 463–4.

[14] Guthrie, "Evangelicals respond," p. 464.

[15] Guthrie, "Evangelicals respond," p. 462.

[16] Guthrie, "Evangelicals respond," p. 464.

[17] Stan Guthrie, "Living death," *World Pulse*, 4 September 1998, p. 1.

[18] Stan Guthrie, "The church grows under Islam's shadow," *Christianity Today*, 15 January 1990, p. 51.

[19] Bill MacLeod, "Cairo's moment?" *World Pulse*, 2 January 1998, pp. 1–2.

[20] "Christians now praying for thousands," *Vision: A View of AWM Media*, Vol. IV/99, p. 2.

[21] "Indonesian revival continues," *World Pulse*, 20 August 1999, p. 7.

[22] Charles R. A. Hoole, "Sri Lanka at 50," *World Pulse*, 17 April 1998, p. 2.

CHAPTER 22

[1] "Muslim president of Sierra Leone meets with World Relief president to praise work of churches" press release, 18 February 2000, p. 2.

[2] Stan Guthrie, "Past midnight," *EMQ*, January 2000, p. 101.

[3] Jay Gary, interview by author via Internet, 9 September 1999.

[4] Gary, *op. cit.*

[5] Guthrie, pp. 103–4.

[6] Paul Borthwick, interview by author via Internet, 17 August 1999.

[7] Guthrie, pp. 101–2.

[8] Borthwick, *op. cit.*

[9] Guthrie, p. 103.

[10] Guthrie, p. 103.

[11] Guthrie, p. 103.

[12] William A. Dyrness, *Learning About Theology from the Third World* (Grand Rapids: Zondervan Publishing House, 1990), p. 28.

[13] David J. Hesselgrave, "What Evangelicals are doing and what Evangelicals should be doing," unpublished paper, n.d.

[14] Guthrie, p. 104.

[15] Guthrie, p. 104.